MAA AANKH

VOLUME II

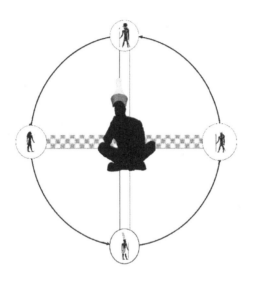

Discovering the Power of I AM
Using the Shamanic Principles of
Ancient Egypt for Self-Empowerment and
Personal Development

Derric "Rau Khu" Moore

Four Sons Publications
Liberal, KS
1solalliance.com

Published by: Four Sons Publications

Contact: 1 SõL Alliance Co.
                   P.O. Box 596
                   Liberal, KS 67905-0596
                   www.1solalliance.com

Disclaimer & Legal Notice

The information contained in this book is intended to be educational and not for diagnosis, prescription, or treatment of any health disorder whatsoever. This information should not replace consultation with a competent healthcare professional. The content of the book is intended to be used as an adjunct to a rational and responsible healthcare program prescribed by a licensed healthcare practitioner. This is a book about faith. As such the author and publisher do not warrant the success any person would have using any of the exercises and techniques contained herein. Success and failure will vary. The author and publisher therefore are in no way liable for any misuse of the material contained herein.

To protect the identity and privacy of others, most of the names within this book have been adapted, modified and changed for confidentiality purposes. Any resemblance to real persons, living or dead is purely coincidental.

Cover art and Illustrations by: Derric "Rau Khu" Moore
Photos courtesy of Dreamstine.com

ISBN: 978-0-9855067-1-1

Printed in the United States of America

MAA AANKH

VOLUME II

**Discovering the Power of I AM
Using the Shamanic Principles of
Ancient Egypt for Self-Empowerment and
Personal Development**

Thanks to Fu-Kiau Bunseki, Ph.D for your inspiring works and insight about the Kongo culture.

Thanks to those ancestors of the past, the present and those in the future, and who have contributed in some way, great and small.

Other Books by the Author:

MAA AANKH Volume I:

Finding God the Afro-American Spiritual Way,

by Honoring the Ancestors and Guardian Spirits

Kamta: A Practical Kamitic Path for Obtaining Power

Maa: A Guide to the Kamitic Way for Personal Transformation

MAA AANKH Volume III:

The Kamitic Shaman Way of Working the Superconscious Mind to

Improve Memory, Solve Problems Intuitively and Spiritually Grow

Through the Power of the Spirits (Volume 3)

Honoring the Ancestors the Kemetic Shaman Way:

A Practical Manual for Venerating and Working with the Ancestors

from a God Perspective

The Kamta Primer: A Practical Shamanic Guide for Using Kemetic

Ritual, Magick and Spirituality for Acquiring Power

En Español: Maa Aankh Volume I:

Encontrando a Dios al Modo Espiritual Afroamericano, Honrando a los

Ancestros y a los Espiritus Guardianes

CONTENTS

INTRODUCTION 1

Chapter 1: Exploring Kamta 11
Our Purpose in Life..16
Beauty in Simplicity 20
Exercise 1: Issuing Commands to the Universe 23

Chapter 2: Who is the Great I AM? 27
Rau: The Divine POWER of I AM..29
Who Are We?..32
Exercise 2: Interpreting Universal Signs.................................33

Chapter 3: Exploring the Three Aspects of Our Awareness............35
The Ba: Our Divine Spark Within 35
The Sahu and Our Garment..38
The Ab and the Human Soul 45
Exercise 3: How to Begin to Cleanse the Soul 51

Chapter 4: How to Defeat the Enemy 55
Exploring the Sahu Further..56
Heaven & Hell Is a State Of Mind 61
Exercise 4: How to Recognize Divine Signs 65

Chapter 5: The Three Paths to Ultimate Power 69
Path of the Deshret Crown: POWER by Struggle & Spirituality 72
Path of the Hedjet Crown: POWER by Consequence & Mysticism.......74
Path of the Pschent Crown: POWER by Resolve & Miracles.......76
We Are All Called..77
Exercise 5: How to Accept the Call...95

Chapter 6: Obtaining Power over Evil 111
Children of Osar versus the Casualties of Set 112
The Spiritual Wickedness in High Places 117
Exercise 6: How to Create a Pschent Talisman.......................139

Chapter 7: Creating a Magical Way of Life.............................151
The Seven Divine Abilities 156
The Gods Were People Too!..159
Working the Kamitic Faith..163
Exercise 7: Creating Sacred Space for You Guardian Spirits 188

Appendix A: Suggested Practices 207

Appendix B: Selected Bibliography 212

INDEX 214

LIST OF FIGURES

Figure 1: Kongo Cross Cosmogram _____ 14

Figure 2: Maa Aankh Cosmogram _____ 15

Figure 3: On the Edge of Two Worlds _____ 18

Figure 4: Red & White Pschent Crown and Yang and Yin Symbol _____ 19

Figure 5: Unified Kingdom_____ 19

Figure 6: Ruler of KAMTA_____ 36

Figure 7: Ruler of TASETT_____ 45

Figure 8: Ruler of the Sun_____ 47

Figure 9: Evolution of Divine Consciousness_____ 48

Figure 10: The Mental State of Hell_____ 62

Figure 11: The Mental State of Heaven _____ 62

Figure 12: The Red Flag of Set_____ 66

Figure 13: The White Flag of Osar_____ 67

Figure 14: Spiritual House for the Aakhu & Netcharu_____ 96

Figure 15: Figa (fee-gah) Hand Gesture for Averting Evil Eye_____ 134

Figure 16: Spiritual Pot for Netcharu with Guides _____ 188

Figure 17: Possible Pot Design for Nebhet_____ 192

"The kingdom of heaven is within you; and whosoever shall know himself shall find it."

– Kamitic (Ancient Egyptian) Proverb

And when he was demanded of the Pharisees, when the kingdom of God should come, he answered them and said, The kingdom of God cometh not with observation: Neither shall they say, Lo here! or, lo there! for, behold, the kingdom of God is within you.

– Luke 17: 20 – 21, KJV

INTRODUCTION

Most of us are familiar with affirmations and have heard that if we repeat an affirmation to ourselves a number of times, that the affirmation has the ability to change our thinking and miraculously change our life. Many of us have even struck up the courage to repeat a few of these affirmations to ourselves like, "I am happy. I am healthy. I am getting better day-by-day. I am prosperous," and so on.

But only a few of us have had success with affirmations. The reason is because when we affirm, "I am happy. I am healthy. I am getting better day-by-day. I am prosperous". There is a small doubting voice that comes to us and says, "That's a lie! You're lying! You're not happy and healthy. You are not getting better, but worst. You will never prosper."

It is this small, annoying, doubting voice that has convinced many of us. That affirmations, either do not work or that they work for only a certain group. The real reason that affirmations and declarations don't work for most people is because when they are repeated. It is through our false self, the "Me" part of our being, and not the higher self, which is the power of I AM.

Every major religion has stated that we are made in the image of God, but when it comes to creating change in our life. We do not proceed from a godly manner. For instance, we try to recover from illnesses, improve our relationships, increase our finances, etc. by reading books, and by listening to the opinions of others (most of whom are not even qualified to give adequate, practical or sound advice). We basically try to create change in our life from a mortal perspective, based upon our anxieties, fears, and worries about the things we have and don't have. We don't approach our problems from a divine perspective by following our intuition, because most of us have been taught. That when we have a problem to run away from it. So that little annoying voice discourages us from achieving greatness because we don't believe that we are like our Creator, a god or goddess.

A lot of religious leaders shy away Genesis 1:26, which states that we are "made in the image of God," because they can't understand that if we are a reflection of those who came before us. How it is possible for us to be a reflection of God. As a result, most skip this particular passage because they don't think it is important, but the fact is that it is the key to understanding who God is and who we are. It is only when we accept that we are gods and goddesses that it becomes clear. That most religious text was written to be a guide and not instruction manuals on how we are supposed to live our life. For instance, in Proverbs 18:21, which states "Life and death are in the power of our tongue," clearly means that we have the same quality (not quantity) of power that God has to create and destroy with our words. This is why, besides God, there is no other being on the planet that has this authority.

What this means is that you can't expect to have abundance, perfect health and happiness, if you talk about lack of, illness and misery, because this is not how a divine being acts, behaves, thinks and speaks. If you want a better life you have to declare it, plan and work towards it.

My Story, My Song

This is a subject that I know about very well because I wrote about it extensively in my first book Maa Aankh volume one. For those who don't know, I am the eldest son born to an Apostolic Pentecostal preaching family. I was born breeched and ever since then as my Mom say I have been "backwards," meaning a little different from the rest. My "differentness" made itself known in my sarcastic humor, in my surreal drawings and the questions I use to ask about God and the bible. It was this "differentness" that caused people to prophesized on me (on more than one occasion) that I was supposed to follow in my father, grandfather and uncles' footsteps, which was to be a preacher, but I saw things different. The reason I didn't follow in their footsteps is because I didn't have a strong connection with God.

You see after the Civil Rights Movements and the present Cultural Movement of the 1970s. The African American community, like the rest of the country, was undergoing a tremendous cultural change. As a result, a lot of people had mixed feelings on existing cultural practices and traditions, as they tried to gain a more secure footing in American society. So, the cultural practices that my grandparents and others in their generation practiced were seen by my parents' generation as being backwards, outdated and silly. As a result, I saw firsthand older people in the church who had the "spirit" or who were "anointed" called upon to pray over others, because they could get prayers answered. But as far as them teaching this unique art to others, it was not done. Instead it was simply stressed to believe in God for one's salvation, get a good education, so that you can get a good job.

Of course, this didn't deter my curiosity in understanding who is God and how can I do the miraculous things that I saw the elders in the church do. So, I tried to learn the old ways anyway because during the mid-1980s when crack cocaine had hit the streets. I didn't want to get caught up in the violence. So, I like so many of my peers got baptized and received the Holy Ghost. For the first few weeks, I felt good and could sense a change, but after that I found myself in situations where I had to mentally and physically fight to avoid *swingin'* (1980s slang for drug peddling) and related crimes.

I didn't want to fight but had no choice, which made me wonder why the Holy Ghost had failed to keep me safe from physical harm. I asked myself, "Was it because God did not want me? Was I not one of the chosen ones destined to go to heaven? Did God not love me?" It wasn't long after, that I lost my Holy Ghost and since I backslid even after trying to be saved, according to teaching I was going to hell. So, logically I decided that if I was going to hell, there was no purpose in living. Frustrate, disgusted, mad at the world and angry as hell with God, I cursed God and called God every name I could in an attempt to provoke him to strike my 13-year-old body down. Then suddenly, after my hour-long tirade, a voice spoke to me and told me to learn about the ancient Egyptians.

Since that time, I studied and read everything I could find that had something to do with the ancient Egyptians in order to become more "spiritual". This led me to studying religion, history, metaphysics, herbal medicine, psychology, and folk traditions and introduced me to the occult. Like most people searching for self but not aware of it, I accumulated a lot of books, but none of what I read made me more feel

3

more spiritual. In fact, many of these books made me even wonder if God was even real. So I joined various study groups and temporarily adopted numerous beliefs based upon theory. For instance, because my grandmother was diagnosed with diabetes and my grandfather was diagnosed with hypertension. Since I read that these ill-nesses run in the family. I worried about getting these conditions or worse, so I changed my diet, exercise regularly and eventually became a vegetarian because I didn't want to become ill. But, in a short while after being involved in several study groups and having to succumb to a number of egos. I learned that being "spiritual" had nothing to do with how much you read, who you know or what you know, but how you live and treat others regardless of their affiliations, beliefs or disabilities. This is when I discovered that unlike the religious teachings of my youth that taught that through baptism and receiving the Holy Ghost you could get to God. I learned that God had been within me all along.

After being in and out of relationships, the most memorable relationship I had where I learned about true love was because I wanted a "spiritual woman" and, this woman I was with claimed that we were "soul mates." After getting into this relationship, which led to me being unemployed and homeless for a couple of years, I learned after the constant arguments, the failed promises and breach of commitment that in order for any relationship to work. The give and take ratio throughout the relationship will fluctuate on occasion to 70/30 but on an average it should be 50/50. If ever it stays at 70/30 for too long or moves to 90/10. There is a problem and no amount of spiritual teaching or training is going to fix it. True love is the only power that gives you the strength to endure in order to address one's conditionings. True love is the only way to make a relationship last but in order to experience true love. All parties involved have to develop it because it has more to do with self-control and less to do with selflessness. This simply means that both have to learn how to compromise their principles for the sake of "Us" instead of "I".

It was also during this time I met a number of spiritual teachers and spiritual workers. The most influential spiritual teacher was a black Cuban man, whom I called Papa, that taught me a lot of valuable lessons that I still refer to, to this day. It was his advice and teachings that would have the most impact on my development because he was

4

the one instrumental in getting me to understand that I can't recreate, reconstruct or repair the past. I can only focus on the present in order to create a better future. Through Papa's words of wisdom, I was able to repair a lot of the damage that had been done to me spiritually by adopting a more holistic perspective to life. Although most of what Papa taught me at the time, like most wisdom teachings, seemed over my head. I still wrote what he told me down in my *libro* (journal) and, it was a good thing I did. The reason is because a few years later, I would need to revisit these teachings in order to save myself, in the future.

Some time had passed since I last talked with Papa. Several years later, I loss two very important people in my life, my grandfather followed by my grandmother a year later, then all of a sudden. After years of eating healthy food, exercising and living a relatively "healthy" lifestyle, I became deathly ill. I had problems, standing for long periods of time. I had problems breathing and I had chest pains. It was horribly scary. It took a while it seemed but, Murphy's Law, which states that if something can go wrong, it is bound to go wrong, seemed to have been activated even though I was trying to be healthy. For a whole year, I was in and out of hospitals and specialty clinics, until finally they diagnosed me as having systemic lupus. The first thoughts that came to me my mind was of course, "How?" and "Why?" considering that no one in my family (or extended family) has ever been diagnosed with this dis-ease. I remembered, one of the first people I talked to was my brother who told me that this situation was about me working my faith. After listening to him and reflecting on my life, that's when I realized that I changed my diet and lifestyle for the wrong reasons.

I didn't change my diet and lifestyle to be healthier. I changed it because I didn't want to become ill. I even remembered telling people that this was the reason I changed my diet and lifestyle. It was out of fear. I know now that you don't create change by focusing on what you don't want, but instead by focusing on what you want.

So, I began the road to recovery by implementing what I had learned and surrounding myself with everything joyful that reminded me about life. Through trial and error I found what worked and what was just, a beautiful, sounding theory. This is when I learned that the best way to use affirmations is by declaring, "I am in perfect health," while imagining what I would do if I was never diagnosed and never became ill in the first place. I got better because I meditated on this image, while repeating this and other declarations during my times of leisure, until they became automatic. After acting like the illness never occurred, in time I began to stand, walk, dance and eventually run again.

I no longer ate certain foods to prevent myself from getting ill. I ate certain foods to "prolong my life," which became my new focus and purpose. I exercised and began engaging in all sorts of activities that were about expressing the joy of life, like writing, drawing, poetry, dancing, etc. I stopped watching and listening to anything that would cause me to become anxious, fearful or worrisome. I stopped worrying about the future and things that I couldn't directly control like politics. When I heard negative news, which is anything that would cause me to become anxious, fearful, disappointed, nervous, worrisome. For instance, like how was my rent going to get paid when I was unable to work. I declared that everything was going to be all right and tried to find ways of getting it paid. I didn't worry or fret, when those thoughts that I was going to be thrown out in the street with my things came to mind. I ignored them and lo' and behold it was paid.

It was during these rough and tough times I discovered for myself that God is omnipotent, omniscient and omnipresent. I believed that God would provide, and I was provided for which revealed to me God's omnipotence. I believed that I would get "blessings" or "lucky breaks" and there were all sorts of favors given to me. Some of these favors I received were from individuals whom I thought were my enemies. Again, it revealed to me God's greatness. I learned first hands that God was omniscient when I received ideas to do certain things and they led to more opportunities.

Today, the lupus ill-ness is in remission. I have already been taken off of several prescriptions and the physician is looking forward to taking me off the last one, here shortly. My life has gotten a hundred times better because I declared the life that I wanted and it was through the power of God in me, that it manifested. I know with utmost certainty because of this experience that I would not have been able to accomplish this feat if I had not changed my thinking. If I had begged and pleaded for God to save me, I surely believe that I would have died because, I had two near death experiences and treaded the dividing line between life and death very closely. I didn't die because I refused to die and decided to activate the divine power that God has infused in all of us, within me.

This experience taught me that if you do not believe that you are made in the image of God. Affirmations and declarations will not work the way you want them to because when you say, "I am." I AM can only become what you declare I AM to be. When I imagined myself and declared that, "I am in perfect health." What happened is that the more I repeated this declaration and imagined doing things that healthy people do. The more I began to believe it, see it and feel it. Eventually, it began to resonate strongly resonated within me and become a physical reality. At first I thought it was magic, but when I applied it over and over again. I concluded that this was a sacred science.

I am telling you this because you may be going through a difficult time in your life right now. For instance, the relationship you put so much time and energy in is not fruitful. You may have been diagnosed with some ill-ness. You lost your job or didn't get the job you were hoping to get. Whatever situation you are in, I encourage you to search your heart and see how your words and thoughts created the life that you are in. If you want good days, you need to declare that, "Every day is a good day because I am alive." If something you want does not work out. You need to declare that, "A greater blessing is in store." It is all about perspective. You have to learn to see the glass as being half–full instead of half–empty, because this is how God sees things. So, you can either look at the situation you are in as a curse or use it to propel your blessings.

Blessings and Curses Come in Cycles

I chose to use the situation I was in to see it as a blessing and even though I never thought about it at the time. When I became ill the whole situation seemed very similar to when I first had problems with understanding God. When I look back at a lot of the situations that I was in I began to notice a similar pattern. For instance, the reason I tried to get deeply involved in the church was to avoid getting caught up in the escalating drug violence occurring in Detroit. The relationship with the "spiritual woman" that taught me about love. The only reason I was in that situation was because I willed myself to do so. When I wanted the situation to end, I declared it so by constantly talking about what I didn't want, didn't like and so on, until the relationship was finally ended. The reason I became ill was because I didn't want to be ill. By I focusing on what I didn't want to occur generated the cycle of curses.

It was while I was ill through my late grandmother I discovered a cosmogram called the Maa Aankh, which helped me to realize that I was in a cycle and that the only way to be reborn from this experience was by creating a new way of life. The reason I had to create a new way of life was because it was the only way to drown out the doubting voice that fought me every time I moved towards bettering and improving my health. Although I am a lot healthier and better, because that annoying voice has for the most part been silenced in regards to this illness. He still exists in the background chatting up a storm about other aspects of my life. This made me realize that wayward thoughts will always come to us, but we give power to them when we dwell and speak them aloud. Every time we speak something aloud especially over a period of time, it not only manifests but also has to cycle until it runs out.

This is why while I am grateful that I survive the experience and the wisdom I have gained because of it. When I reflect back on how all of this began and how if I knew what I know now I would have made some different decisions. I concluded that a lot of what I had experienced could have been avoided had I been taught the spiritual system of my elders. The decision not to teach my generation and those following after has created a major spiritual deficit, which has led to a host of deviate behavior because of a lack of spiritual guidance. For many being "spiritual" means living any kind of way you choose so long as you believe in God. The whole aspect behind consequences for ones actions has been thrown out of the window. It is for this reason; everyone is claiming to be "spiritual" while homicide rates amongst the youth is steadily climbing, heinous crimes are being committed by our elected officials and the world seems to be spiraling to its doom. Our ancestors and elders faced much dire situations than we had but they not only survived, some of them were able to prosper all because of their spiritual tradition.

I live today as a testimony to the power of our ancestors' knowledge and wisdom of God. I have a very strong conviction and a working rapport with the Divine. I didn't just get this by repeating affirmations and declarations. It came about because I got a total change in consciousness through my ancestral spiritual tradition. This is what I believe we need today to empower us. This is the reason I wrote this book. To help us to return to the old ways of working with the Spirit, but at the same time preserve it and prevent it from becoming a cultural fad or a do-it-yourself trendy system, as so many vital practices have become in the Western culture. This is the purpose behind exploring this from a shamanistic perspective. It is the approach that those who were "anointed" in our life used to created change.

Through this book, I hope and pray that you find much pleasure and understanding from reading it, as I have in writing it. It has been very therapeutic for me.

God Bless you,
Derric "Rau Khu" Moore

How to Use This Book

People from all walks of life are interested in miracles. No one wants to live in poverty, be ill, be seen as failure or not be loved, so we all seek the divine in order to ensure that these conditions don't occur. But far too often most writers focus on the problem and not the solution. They write about how a problem occurred and how to prevent it from reoccurring, but rarely do they discuss why and the lesson to be learned from it. This is what makes this book unique, because it has been specifically designed to help you to achieve tangible positive results in your life by first exploring the relationship between the two most important entities in our universe – the Spirit of God and the divine spark within us all.

When we are in alignment with the Infinite Spirit of God through our spirit, not only can we resolve our problems, but we can also safely meet our spirit guides, summon our spiritual guardians, recall dreams and past lives, from a clearer, more powerful and safer perspective, because we have tapped into our divinity. This is why throughout the book I use the term God interchangeably with Spirit and the Divine, because I recognize that God is beyond our one-dimensional thinking.

Because information is good, but application is better. There are a number of exercises discussed within these pages to help you to apply the concepts based upon the understanding that the way to impress an idea upon our subconscious mind. We have to use a host of symbols (including but not excluding metaphors, songs, colors, gestures, images, music, etc.), which is the basis of miracles or what some refer to as magic.

It is for this reason, after rereading this book I am aware that on more than one occasion I have repeated certain concepts. This was done deliberately to reinforce the point. I have found that the more we reread a concept, the stronger the impression is made and helps us to remember the idea. Again, I encourage you not to take what has been read at face value but review it, study it and try it. It is the only way you can know if it will benefit you.

Chapter 1:
Exploring Kamta

Quiet as kept when Europeans enslaved the Africans and brought them to the Americas. A new form of spirituality was introduced to the Western hemisphere. In North America, the Protestant Christian doctrine resonated strongly with early African Americans during the First Great Awakening, because they identified with the biblical characters and saw themselves as the persecuted people of the bible. Using shamanistic technique brought from Africa, early African Americans created what Theophus "Thee" Smith calls a Conjuring Culture[1], which is a "magical means of transforming reality." It was this new religious tradition that allowed them to conjure the strength to persevere, preserve their humanity and maintain their insanity, during slavery and the Jim Crow segregation era. While I might add, living in a society where they were treated and constantly told they, were less than human.[2]

Unfortunately, like most of the shamanic systems of the world, a greater portion of this spiritual tradition was suppressed by the government and various religious organizations, which is why the very mention of anything African related summons images of spooky witchdoctors and silly ideas of orgiastic voodoo curses. Most of what remains today of the original African American spiritual system can be either found in two places: One, in the church superficially practiced with no true comprehension. Two in colored bottles sold in novelty shops and online stores, by people unfamiliar with the original culture touting to others fascinated by the idea that they can curse their enemy with no repercussion. That anyone can use this system regardless of his and her belief and lifestyle.

When I finally met an elder spiritual worker, I learned that this was not their spiritual way. They didn't do a lot of dabbling based upon

---

[1] *Conjuring Culture: Biblical Formations of Black America (Religion in America)* by Theophus H. Smith

[2] This voice of discouragement sounds very much like the doubting and discouraging voice we met earlier. In the future we will identify who and what this discouraging voice is.

theories written in books many times because they couldn't afford to buy them. They relied upon God and their intuition, which led me to conclude that the reason this tradition wasn't passed down, is because. The original African American mystical science that birthed this unique spiritual tradition was not discussed in the church anymore. As a result, many Black churches simply "loss the Spirit" and also loss the "anointing," which is the reason I (and a host of others in my generation) left the church in favor of "spirituality". Proof of this can be seen in the fact that before the 1980s crack epidemic, it was uncommon to hear of so many people not attending church as it is today. Most contemporary churches in the minds of many, who remember religious service prior to this period, see church as a place to attend on Sunday in order to be entertained because it has no "Spirit" or "soul". It is lifeless and most of the services are extremely faddish to say the least.

Please understand that I am not in any way ridiculing or criticizing these institutions nor am I advocating that people attend church. I am also not implying that people who attend church are mindless drones. The fact is that something is missing and anyone that pays attention can see it. It can be heard in the music especially when you compare songs sung by Mahalia Jackson, like *How I Got Over*, to the songs sung today. If you agree there is no comparison, then you can sense the loss. The purpose of this discourse is to illustrate how a change in awareness occurred. This is why it is so widely believed that African Americans being the farthest from Africa completely loss their culture due to slavery, which is purely a myth. What was loss is the theology and understanding behind our cultural tradition because it doesn't coincide precisely with Western religious thinking, hence the bible. If it had, African Americans would not have survived slavery, because of early American biblical beliefs and teachings about the curse of Ham.

This is why early African Americans conjured a new religious tradition. In order to understand and appreciate African American (and for that matter all Afro-Atlantic) spiritual traditions, it has to be first understood that an enslaved and destitute people created this spiritual system out of the sheer need to survive. These abused and battered people who refused to be "broken" through verbal, mental, spiritual and physical abuse, met in the fields and other clandestine settings, to practice their spirituality in secret, as a form of resistance and to avoid opposition from the slaveholders and policing officials. It was these horrendous conditions of adversity that inspired early African Americans to develop a powerful healing tradition with its own mystical teachings, herbal science, healing arts like the laying of hands, divination practices and code of ethics. That birthed the numerous practices that exist today such as speaking in tongues, laying in hands, prophetic visions, and warrior praying (the so-called prayer warriors, no pun intended) and so on.

African American spirituality was born out of resistance because it was heavily influenced by the Kongo philosophy. This was mainly due to the fact that the Kongo people were the first Africans brought to North America and although other ethnic groups were taken from Africa to North America. The Kongo people were also the largest and therefore the most influential[3]. Proof of this fact from the memory jars[4] found in the Appalachia mountains to the cemeteries where slaves were buried, has been found all throughout the southeast of United States where slave communities existed. As a result, the glue that bound the early spiritual system together in Protestant North America was the Kongo Cross[5].

The Kongo Cross (also called the Yowa), which was foundation of Kongo-Angolan society, served as the foundation of early African American spirituality and gave rise to such traditions as the ring shout,

---

[3] It is also believed that the Kongo people were the most influential because unlike the other Africans, they had some knowledge of Roman Catholicism because they were the first to encounter Europeans prior to the advent of slavery. Upon doing so many of them voluntarily converted to the Christian faith based upon religious similarities and syncretism.

[4] Research has found that memory jars also called forget-me-not jug, ugly jars, whatnot jars and spirit jars originated from the BaKongo culture and were placed in cemeteries as a grave marker and way of remembering the deceased.

[5] For more on this see *Flash of the Spirit: African & Afro-American Art& Philosophy* by Robert T. Farris.

an ecstatic dance that was once practiced by slaves in the United States, and is still practiced in the Caribbean.

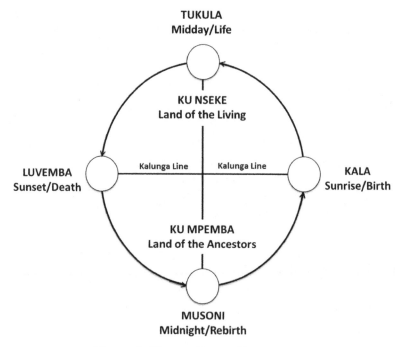

Figure 1: Kongo Cross Cosmogram

It was this cosmogram that encouraged early African Americans to adopt and borrow foreign influences, in order to use them as tools of resistance and survival. As a result, the old time healers didn't have a host of store bought items (like people do today), which they used to achieve a desired result. All they had was the bare essentials, which they found around their dwelling because they were poor and desperate, so they had no choice but to depend and attuned themselves to nature. This is how prayer warriors, the laying of hands and other shamanistic techniques came about, but as previously mentioned this tradition was suppressed in part because it incited insurrection. However, the real reason this spiritual system fell into obscurity is because the original African theology that existed in the United States had been lost[6], making it virtually impossible for anyone to discover this path.

---

[6] Also, because the Kongo people were the first to encounter the

14

Thankfully, as Michael Harner the author of *The Way of the Shaman*, notes, it doesn't matter how far removed we are from our ancestral past. We can still reconnect to ancestral roots because we are all the indigenous descendants of some group that walked the earth. This means we don't have to travel to another country in order to learn how to implement spiritual principles in our life, and. We don't have to imitate or mimic anyone because shamanism is not a religion that is owned, managed or operated by one culture, group or people.

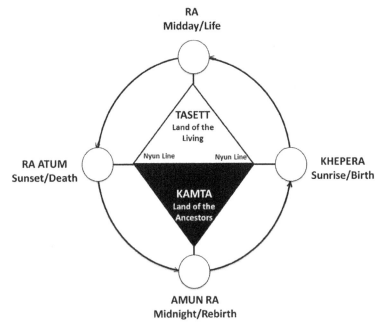

Figure 2: Maa Aankh Cosmogram

All we have to do is reconnect to the divine spark dwelling within and it will show us how to retrieve our ancestral wisdom. This is

Portuguese, after the advent of slavery, the Kongo became the first country to be invaded and devastated by colonization, thereby destroying most of the spiritual teachings that were present. To this day important Kongo artifacts are not in the possession of the Kongo people but lie in museums or on some mantle as a showpiece in another country.

what I did because when I became ill. I had no one to assist and coach me back to optimal health. There was no priesthood, no community or anything like that. There was only God, and me and I traced these shamanistic roots back to Kamit, which is how I discovered the Maa Aankh cosmogram and thereby conjured Kamta.

Our Purpose in Life

The Maa Aankh is a very important tool because as mentioned previously, the lack of African theology is what led to the early African American spiritual system's demise. But, by using the Maa Aankh as a guide, I was able to return to my ancestral roots, reclaim my spiritual heritage and retrieve my "anointing" as others (like the Jews, Native Americans and many others have done within their own cultural traditions).

The general understanding of the Maa Aankh is that our universe consists of two polar energies: aggressive and passive forces. Our universe is full of duality: head and tail, right and left, hot and cold, up and down, male and female, young and old, etc., which can be found everywhere.

The hustle and bustle of daily life particularly when the sun is shining during the day hours corresponds to the aggressive aspect of nature. However, when the sun has set and everything in general is at rest, this corresponds to the cool and passive aspects of nature. Anything that is active, bustling with energy, physically visible, physically vibrant and extremely extroverted is considered aggressive – called shu (the Kamitic yang), while anything that was passive, reflective, contemplative, invisible and introverted corresponded to tefnut (the Kamitic yin).

Both forces in Kamitic thinking are interdependent upon each other, because they are cosmic twin brother and sister or also described as being husband and wife, but neither is stronger or weaker than the other. Nor are these forces considered to be good, bad or vice versa. They are simply the dual forces that exist in our universe in order to sustain life, but the cycle of life began according to Kamitic philosophy from a state of rest. Since, life first emerged from a passive state, like from an egg, or from the womb of a woman. It was generally accepted that everything first emerged from the invisible, spiritual realm, which is called KAMTA[7] to the visible, physical realm called TASETT.

Managing tefnut and shu in our daily life is an everyday affair. Since both forces are needed in order to maintain the Circle of Life, whenever either one of these two forces becomes too polarized it creates imbalance. Therefore, by seeing the KAMTA and TASETT relationship in everything we are able to maintain order in our life. For instance, imagine if you are in a heated discussion that takes a turn and becomes an argument. Usually, when we are in this situation where we hear another arguing with us. We naturally tend to become annoyed, agitated, restless and stressed because the situation is hot, full of active energy, vibrant emotions, and full of shu energy. If you give into the annoyance, agitation or stress and respond by arguing with the individual, you have just caused the whole situation to tip towards TASETT, thus creating an imbalance, which could possibly lead to a fight.

By staying calm and silent instead of offering a rebuttal, you have just imbued the heated situation with cooling tefnut energies, thus creating balance returning back to KAMTA. As a result, the possible fight that was soon to erupt has been defused.

Aggression and physical force are needed in order to survive in this physical world, but passive and spiritual forces are needed to live a happy and peaceful life. So, the red Deshret crown is used to symbolize TASETT, while the white Hedjet[8] crown is used to symbolize KAMTA.

---

[7] KAMTA is an Old Kingdom term, which was also called the Duat or Tuat (12 Hours of Night) and Amenta (the heavens).
[8] The white Hedjet crown was also known as the crown of Narmer, the first ruler to unify Kamit.

17

Red Deshret Crown   **White Hedjet Crown**

Historically, TASETT was the Old Kingdom name of Lower Kamit, and KAMTA was the Old Kingdom name of Upper Kamit. When the two crowns were worn together, they formed one single crown called the Pschent crown symbolizing the unification of Ancient Egypt.

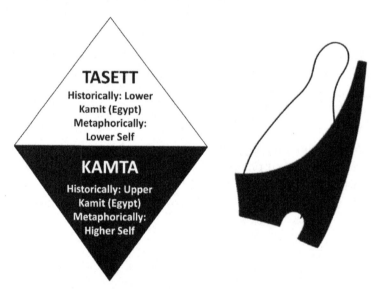

Figure 3: On the Edge of Two Worlds

Metaphorically speaking KAMTA symbolizes the higher self or higher division of our spirit, while TASETT symbolizes the lower self or lower division of our spirit. When both crowns were worn as one, they symbolized the unification of kingdom (higher and lower divisions of our spirit or self) within and our ability to live in harmony with nature, which is very similar to the Chinese yang and yin symbol.

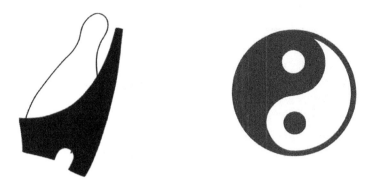

Figure 4:
Red & White Pschent Crown and Yang and Yin Symbol

Our objective in life is to learn how to unify and maintain the unity of our kingdom by tapping into the higher or upper division of our spirit, hence the name of the tradition, Kamta.

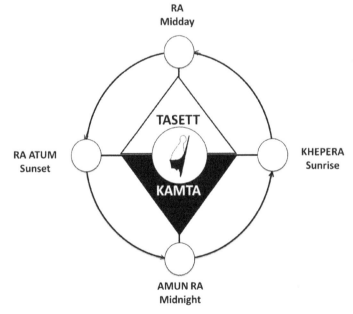

Figure 5: Unified Kingdom

Beauty in Simplicity

Spirituality is not supposed to be difficult. The reason it seems so is because selfish men have viciously promoted their own agenda using religion, which has confused the greater population's understanding about God. As a result, most people today live their life by blind faith instead of actually having a knowing of who and what God is in his or her life, thus the reason for most of the problems that exist in our world today. Proof of this fact can be found in history, which reveals that prior to the rise of organized religions. Spiritual traditions were local and usually confined to one's geographical location. Ancient men and women didn't just go around worshipping rocks and trees the way some archeologists, historians and theologians would like people to believe. Early humans were very much like people are today, concerned with understanding how "things" worked. They didn't just create spiritual systems (or religions) for the fun of it. A spiritual tradition was created based upon their practical experience to help them to better understand the world around them and themselves. If the system didn't make sense and didn't work, it was abandoned, but if it helped people to understand their environment and to better their life. The system was cherished.

So, if a spiritual concept spread and was adopted in a foreign region. It had to be because the spiritual system worked, which is why whole fragments of the Kamitic traditions have been found south of present-day Egypt in the land occupied by the Kushites (ancient Nubians) and as far north as Greece and Rome. It is the same reason why Kamitic concepts and ideas have been found throughout the Christian doctrine. It is because during the times of antiquity, Kamit dominated the ancient world scene because she had the oldest and most reliable spiritual system. It should be noted that during these times, men didn't war and use religion as a weapon of war, people didn't kill in the name of some deity, and women were cherished (even though they may not have had equal rights as men except in Kamit) mainly because they were seen as being the epitome of the female divinity, thus providing for the people as nature does for its inhabitants, hence Mother Earth.

20

But, when organized religion came about, so began the saving of souls with religious text in one hand and the sword (or some other weapon) in the other. It is interesting that while the purpose of religion according to the origin of the word was to unite humanity for a higher purpose. Nothing in the history of the world has caused more confusion, destruction, separation and mass bloodshed than organized religion. This is why the great thing about shamanic spiritual practices is that:

- They are not based upon dogma but upon principles. Principles like the natural law of gravity, have an influence on us all regardless who we are, where we are and if we believe in it or not.

- They are not based upon blind faith but upon wisdom and experience.

- One cannot convert to a shamanic spiritual tradition nor are you obligated to follow it. You are either called and you accept it or you don't.

- They are not governed by political correctness and other contemporary values but by ancestral taboos because it predates modernity.

- It respects all religious paths because it is not polarized and will adapt from them to obtain the wisdom needed to achieve a goal.

For this reason, I meant for this book to be both lighthearted and profound because spirituality has been made to be a boring and laborious chore. We should all look forward to connecting with the Divine in order to change undesirable aspects of our life, but we don't because many of us think of spirituality as consisting of just meditating in the lotus position pursuing lofty goals like enlightenment. I personally think that if that is what you want to do with your life by all means, but I find more joy in pursuing more tangible goals by using the divine power. For instance, if I can improve the relationship between my spouse and me by using the power of God versus spiritual enlightenment, I would look forward to doing this more so than just trying to get enlightenment, because if my wife is happy, my household is happy.

This approach works because it is based upon the principles of Kamitic (Ancient Egyptian) philosophy and shamanism, which indicates that people are more engaging with the Divine if we include the Divine in our daily affairs. In other words, if there is a tangible result that can be achieved by using spiritual practices, such as getting gainful employment, improved health, increased finances, etc. by applying principles and adhering to ancestral taboos. One is more inclined to use them versus using them to just merge one's consciousness because there is a vested interest. The failure to use spiritual practice in achieving "mundane" goals is the reason people see obtaining even our most basic necessities that we need to live, like money as evil; instead of seeing that by obtaining money honestly is being spiritual. This is the reason why the Kamitic spiritual systems did not distinguish between mundane and spiritual goals because they understood that everything that we are interested in, the Divine is as well.

Discussed in this book, is not only the scientific theory behind creating miraculous change with your mind but also exercises on how to do it. All the techniques within these pages are based upon the author's personal experience. Through this book you will be able to create changes like our ancestors with the bare essentials by just gathering what you need outside your door.

However, it is important to that this is not to say that the life that we want is going to be created with a set of magical hands that will come out of the ether and make things appear. Nor am I implying that by twinkling our noses like the fictional character Samantha did in the television series *Bewitch* that the things we want will magically fall in place. But, if we were to learn how to hold an image in our mind with certainty, whatever we desire will become a physical reality through the power of I AM. This is how our ancient ancestors lived their life and through this book you can learn how to do the same.

Exercise 1:
Issuing Commands to the Universe

The ability to lay hands and pray as a warrior begins by tapping into your own divine power. To become familiar with your own divine power, you need to learn how to make declarations and speak with authority. The easiest way to learn how to do this is through prayer. Now, there are a lot of explanations on what prayer is and is not, and I have found. The reason most people don't believe or feel they can pray is because they don't know how to get to the Throne of God (the right frame of mind or trance); so that they feel that their prayers are being heard and will be answered.

This is why I prefer to think of this process as Enter into KAMTA, which is simply a shifting of awareness consisting of us not intellectualizing. Viewed from this perspective, prayer simply means talking to the Divine and the spirits that exist in the invisible realm. When we don't think this way, praying to God takes on a real superficial tone and we don't get our prayers answered. I discovered this when I was younger, after noticing that when I got angry and just spoke my mind to God. That is when I had my greatest moments of clarity. I didn't realize this in the beginning but it came to me after hitting rock bottom several times. For me to figure out that what God wants is for us to talk from the heart.

Since my discovery, I talk to God on a regular basis by just speaking my mind when I am alone in the house, the car, on the street, the corner, in front of a tree, etc. because the Divine is everywhere. It is our perspective that makes us see differently. When we change our perspective we see that we can be real because we are not trying to impress anyone. To have more meaningful conversations with God, you have to talk to God as if the Divine is right in front of you. To help you to enter into KAMTA (or the Throne of the Divine), try reciting the Lord's Prayer and/or Psalms 23rd, which are particularly popular for this reason. Repeat these prayers as often as you like, until you develop within you the conviction to pray as you desire.

23

Once you become comfortable with entering into KAMTA. The simplest prayer that you can say is "Thank you" for everything that you are pleased with in your life. By expressing your gratitude for what you are grateful for, you create a feeling of happiness within. Once you have experienced joy from expressing your gratitude. You are ready to move on to having a conversation with the Divine.

For blessings you cannot sound like you are begging. You must speak with authority because this is the only way you can truly express your faith. Pray also for others. Ask that your family, loved ones and friends be blessed. Pray for your coworkers. Send blessings to others by lifting your hands and feel the divine energy passing through you and out of your hands to them. If the individual is not in front of you, simply imagine sending the energy to them. Understand that more people you bless, the more you will be blessed.

It is important that you understand that because we are all made in the image of God. What's important to you is also important to God. God is interested in everything that you are interested in, so we have to stop thinking like mortals and begin to think as God by understanding that everything that exists in our life is for a reason. For instance, it is foolish to believe that money is the root of all evil. Without money, we would not be able to live because the world functions on currency. God is the one that created money and if it is evil, it is only because we are not using it properly. Money like everything else that the Divine has created can be used for constructive or destructive purposes, similar to how fire. If you don't know how to use money or a thing properly, don't condemn and curse it. Ask for wisdom. To begin to use these things for specific purposes, begin by stating your intentions from a divine perspective by using command words.

Command words are very powerful especially when combined with natural items like oil, water or candles of a particular color, because they combine the power of prayer with your intention. Here is a listing of common command words that you might choose to use along with the appropriate colors:

24

- "Clear!" "Conquer!" "Defeat!" "Protect!" and "Remove!" works when asking God to remove obstacles especially me obstruction that are preventing progress. Associated color is **red**.

- "Bless!" "Repeat!" "Refresh" and "Renew" are command words that can be used to increase one's happiness, improve relationships, friendships and love. The general color used for this is white, but works exceptionally well with the color **green**.

- "Absorb!" and "Release!" are commands words used to create miraculous outcomes out of grim situations. The color associated with these command terms is **black**, which draws it strength from KAMTA. Just for clarity, the color black does not necessarily mean evil. All colors and powers are neutral and can be used for either constructive or destructive works.

- "Enlighten", "Purify", and "Balance!" "Bless!" and "Heal!" are command terms used for recovering from an ill-ness, increasing one's knowledge and understanding, as well as their wisdom. The color associated with this command term is the color **white**. Used in general for blessings and as an offering.

- "Clear!" and "Remove!" are the commands used to remove stubborn and gloomy emotions. The color associated with this command in **pink**, which is used for attraction, promoting clean living and romance.

- "Assist!" "Chase!" "Drive!" "Break!" "Banish!" and "Destroy!" are all power commands for control, domination and mastery. The color associated with these commands is **purple**; also the color red can be used.

- "Attract" "Direct!" "Draw!" "Focus!" and "Open!" are all commands associated with the color **orange** and used to create opportunities, change plans and perceive the future events.

- "Balance!" when used with the color **brown** is used to bring a sense of stability to one's physical plane and settling disputes over natural resources, hence court matters.

- "Expand!" and "Empower!" are commands for promoting healing, creating peace, joy and harmony. It is associated with the color **blue (royal blue)** symbolizing the sea's ability to quench fires.

- "Inspire!" and "Devote!" associated with the color **light blue** is used to give a feeling of tranquility, inspiration and devotion.

- "Adapt!" "Bend!" "Center!" "Create!" "Chase Away!" and "Open!" are all commands that correspond to the color **yellow** and the rays of the sun. It can be used to invoke creativity, harmony, imagination and attraction.

This can be employed a number of ways. For instance, to make a room more calm and relaxed, you can pray and imagine a green light encircling you as others come in contact with. You could take a black pebble, tell it your problems, ask it to remove your problems from your life and then cast it over your shoulder away from, while thanking it and walking away with full confidence that God has removed the obstacle. You can take a white candle and issue a prayer for a loved one to be healed, then transfer your request to the candle by spitting into your hands three times (similar to how little boys do to get a grip before climbing something) and rub the candle vigorously in your hands, the lighting it. You can protect your dwelling using red cayenne pepper or wear a certain color to influence your day. You can talk to plants, animals, trees, buildings, money, etc. The ways of using this spiritual technology as you can see are endless.

Please note that if you are using candles there are two things that must considered and that is if you are attracting or repelling something in your life. If you are attracting something, carve what you want i.e. love, money, etc. into the candle. Then take virgin olive oil while holding a mental image of what you want and apply it to the bottom on one side.

Next rub it to the center of the candle. Do the same on the other end by applying oil to the top and stopping at the center.

To repel something apply the oil to the center and rub it downward to the bottom. Then do the same for the other end. Remember to never burn candle unattended and away from flammable objects.

Chapter 2:
Who is the Great I AM?

Prior to the Civil Rights and Cultural Movements in the United States, the most influential and intriguing biblical story to most African Americans was the conversation between Moses and the Great I AM, but who really is I AM?

If you have ever attended any religious service, heard any religious program, listen to any religious poems, prayers or songs, you know that God is described as being the most omnipotent (all-powerful), omniscient (all-knowing) and omnipresent (ever present) being in existence. God is called the Great Almighty, the Provider, the Lord of Everything, but what does this really mean? If you have never experienced any of this with God, then all of these descriptions just give a definition of who God is but not a true understanding of who is God. It is sort of like, if you have never had an apple. I can tell you it is a piece of fruit that grows off a tree, which is red, green, yellow, and can be firm, mushy, sweet or tart. In your mind, you will still not know what an apple is until you have experienced it. It is only after eating seeing, observing and tasting several apples from all over the country and the world that you can truly say, "I know what an apple is."

Well, the same applies to God. How can you describe something that you have never physically seen, heard or touched? It is impossible because God is the most unimaginable, indescribable and incomprehensible Being in existence. So ancient writers used a lot of metaphors to help people to fathom the mystery of God. One of the greatest metaphors was that of the biblical Moses seeing the backside of God, which changed Moses' physical appearance alluding to the idea that Moses was humbled and forever a changed man. This is an allegory referring to the greatness of God, which is why the first truth that we must recognize and accept in order to understand God. Is that God is unimaginable, indescribable and incomprehensible. When you accept and recognize this spiritual fact, it will humble you and prepare you for the awesomeness of who is God by raising your awareness.

This is why I favor Kamitic philosophers name for God, whom they called Nebertchar, which means the Lord of Everything. It pretty much sums up who and what God is by saying that even before you can think of it. God is. Here lies the key to being able to create a miraculous life and bring about positive change. You have to see God truly as an Infinite Source of Power. As long as you continue to see God as being a vengeful and oppressive deity with laws demanding that you worship him or else suffer the consequences. Your awareness will continue to be on a low – TASETT - frequency and you will never see the full glory of God. It is only when you begin to see that God cannot be put into a box and isn't just in a temple. Is when you begin to comprehend that God is truly everywhere. Once you humbly accept that God Is, this is when you will see the backside of God.

Seeing The Beauty of God for Self

Most of what we know about God is actually beliefs that we have learned from others. They are loose definitions but none of them totally describe who and what God is. To know whom God is, if we look back before we were born, before our parents and grandparents were born. If we look further back in time before the shaping of this country, the rise of the various nations and the birth of civilization. If we go further back before life roamed the planet, and even before the planet was created and had formed. Meaning if we reduce everything that exist to its subatomic level, which is smaller than atoms, electrons and the subatomic particles called quarks – that scientist have calculated is the speed of light squared. We find at the smallest subatomic level there is "energy."

This energy is not like the crude energy we use to fuel our cars and heat our homes. It is far more powerful and beyond that. It cannot be created or destroyed. When it ends, simultaneously it begins and vice versa like the big bang. It is divine energy and what this means is that everything that physically exists and will come into physical existence. Comes from this invisible, non-physical or non-material energetic force, which created all of the physical things that exist including our selves.

30

Think about that for a moment. Think about how the same energy that created the universe and the planets within it is also responsible for bringing forth life through the womb of a woman.

Now, contemplate this. If the same energy that produced all of these things in the universe, is also responsible for producing all of the life on the planet; this also means that this infinitely small and all-powerful energy that is beyond our perception is Power or the Spirit of the Divine.

The Power of God is no-thing, but at the same time every-thing because it all comes from God. God is omnipresent (everywhere) because the essence of God exists in all things. God is omniscient (all-knowing) because since God exists in all things, God knows and sees everything. God is omnipotent (all-powerful) because if God exists in all things and knows everything. Obviously, God has control or power over everything as well. This is why God is God or called the Great I Am.

If we keep in mind that everything that exists on a subatomic level is energy that is beyond our physical perception, vibrates at an exceptionally high rate and produces particles that form physical matter. It can be concluded that God is the non-material Source of All of Things that functions on a very high vibrational level, which means everything that physically exists vibrates at a much slower rate. This divine energy, the Spirit or Power of the God that everything comes from is what the Chinese call Chi or Ki. It is what Christians refer to as the Spirit of God, but the Kamitic philosophers in an effort to better understand this awesome power of God, personified it and gave it human qualities. Then they called the Power of God, Ra, Re or Rau.

Rau: The Divine POWER of I AM

Imagine that it is wintertime or that is cold outside and you go to an old house that has a furnace on. The furnace is very hot, so hot that you can't even approach it. You can't put your hands on it because if you do it would physically burn you, but you can admire it from afar. You can also benefit from the heat that it generates from a distance as well.

31

This is how it is when we approach God. Physically we can't touch or even see God, but we know that God exist because we can sense God's Spirit and POWER like the heat from a furnace all around us. The POWER and Spirit of God is called the Rau.

Rau is the Divine Power behind the Sun, but since it is difficult to picture this is our mind. Rau was often symbolized as the sun and used as a metaphor, to express consciousness and human beings longing for fulfillment. Just like a ray of sunlight hits a bead of rainwater and the sunbeam bends into the colors of a rainbow. Rau was imagined as containing every conceivable form of pleasure we all desired including joy, sex, good health, peace, prosperity, passion and love. Rau is the divine power that stirs us up in the morning and motivates us to get out of bed. It is the same divine force that activates our immune system and gives us motivational drive.

Since the Rau is divine in nature, it communicates to us intuitively. When an individual is happy, at peace, full of love and joy. The Rau expresses itself as a high vibration with a very strong brilliance like the sun, thus meaning the individual has a lot of Rau. On the other hand, if an individual is angry, sad, depressed, etc. They have a low vibration, a dull radiance, dim light or a very low amount of Rau.

Divine Power is Eternal

But Rau is not temporal joy. Rau is not a physical high that lasts 5 – 15 minute and then brings us crashing to the ground like a bad energy drink or drugs. Rau is not a moment of ecstasy that is good for the moment but doesn't produce a change in character or convey love. Rau is not a fleeting romance or a brief passionate moment with our spouse of 25 years or longer. Rau is eternal Joy.

No one wants be happy sometimes. We want to be happy all of the time. We don't want our family, friends and colleagues just to like us when they want something from us. We want them to like us all of the time. One of the reasons so many young adults try to avoid marriage is because no one wants to be in a marriage where sexual relations are regulated like food during a famine, or romance occurs only on anniversaries. We all want our needs and wants satisfied on a continuous basis.

So, why is it that things can give us a temporary feeling of joy? Why is that foods likes chocolate or deserts that give us sugar rushes, give us a little joy? Why can't we get a continuous amount of joy from drugs, sex or relationships? It is because since everything that physically exists comes from the Divine's Rau. It has a little "ra" – spiritual power, which is why it provides a temporary joy.

Rau is eternal love, self-control, freedom, health, prosperity, relief from fear and anxiety, personal fulfillment, wisdom, contentment, peace of mind, and much, much more, which are intangible attributes that cannot be obtained by anything in this world. They are all ethereal in nature because the only one that can satiate our desires is Rau. I hope that you can see that this is not some New Age concept that was just created. Just about every culture has described this awesome power that exists all around and within us. This is why the early Christians called the Rau the Holy Spirit, and said upon receiving it that it will provide you with *"wisdom, understanding, counsel, strength, knowledge, Godliness and fear of God"* (Isaiah 11:1-2).

So that we are clear Rau is not the sun, but the Divine Power that emanates from God, like rays from the sun. Just like we cannot physically touch a hot furnace with our hand, yet we can feel the heat being emitted from it. We cannot conceive the totality of God but we can sense God's awesomeness through the Divine's Rau.

But when our needs and wants aren't fulfilled in a timely manner. Most of us become anxious and worried. In fact, if some of our needs have been fulfilled. We see it as a blessing, but we quickly prepare for the day when the blessing will end, as if blessings only arrive during a famine. Other times when we get a need fulfilled, we look at the blessing as a miracle or something too good to be true. Again, out of fear we prepare for the day when the blessing will end.

The truth of the matter is that understanding that Rau is eternal means that it will never end. Therefore, the reason we become unhappy, anxious, fearful or worried when our wants aren't fulfilled when we want them is because we have disconnected ourselves from the Rau.

Since, no one in his or her right mind wants to be miserable in life because we all want the same thing, which is eternal joy. This means the disconnection from Rau most likely was done inadvertently and the reason it occurred is because we don't know how to connect or disconnect to the Rau at will. Therefore in order to connect back to God's Rau we have to understand who we are and our relationship to the Divine.

Who Are We?

So, who are we? What really is, man and woman? Well, one of the most profound, yet most bewildering and controversial scriptures in the bible is Genesis 1:26, which states, "Let us make man in our image." This scripture is the key to understanding who we are and our relationship to God, but usually it is difficult to understand because this concept is commonly glossed over. If we keep in mind who God is and what is God's divine power. Then it is obviously who are or who we are supposed to be.

One way I heard this concept explained was if you make an apple pie and gave a slice to someone to eat. What kind of pie are they eating? The answer obviously is apple pie. If you take the same slice, cut it into fourths and distributed it to three more people, what kind of pie are they eating? Although, it is a smaller piece it is still apple pie. If we took those four pieces, cut them into smaller bite size pieces and again distributed it amongst more people. What would these people taste? Again, it is apple pie and the reason is because it didn't matter how small we reduced the pie. It never changed the essence of the thing. This means that if God is No-Thing and we were created in God's image. Our true essence is also no-thing, because we are all basically a piece of God.

Knowing that we are a piece of the Infinite God composed of divine energy or Rau, which cannot be created or destroyed. Our birth and death only governs our physical being and not our true essence because our true essence or soul is eternal like God's. We therefore, are

34

an exact reflection of God because our soul gives us the right to choose and express our divinity.

Understand there is no other being on the planet like man and woman. No other living being on the planet has the ability to do whatsoever he or she chooses except for man and woman. Like God who vibrates in his highest and purest form in the non-physical but chooses to create an infinite amount of things that seem separate and disconnected from one another. Besides God, there is only one other being that can accomplish the same feat on a smaller scale and that is Man and Woman.

It is the human soul that gives us the ability to choose to connect or disconnect to the Rau. This leads us to conclude that when we are connected to the Rau. Everything is going well and our needs are being fulfilled because we have chosen to do something that aligns us with the Divine's Power. When things are going awry, we obviously are disconnected from the Rau due to some decision we have made.

Exercise 2:
Interpreting Universal Signs

Man and woman therefore, are the sum total of all of creation, which is why in every creation story. After everything was created human beings, come into existence. Connecting with Rau – God's Divine Power, begins by first becoming aware of how this energy manifests itself in our life. Part of the reason many of us don't recognize God's power is because we are wound up, angry and caught up in the everyday life of the world. God is not wound up. God does not get angry, which means in order to see God's Power we have to raise our awareness to where God is. One of the simplest ways to accomplish this is by meditating.

Meditation is not as difficult as some make it seems. Meditation simply means, "to contemplate." The simplest way to meditate is to begin by relax your body and letting go of all the tension in your muscles. Next allow your mind to run free by ignoring all thoughts and

35

ideas to enter into your awareness. In fact, don't think about anything. Just follow the advice of Franz Kafka:

> You do not need to leave your room. Remain silent at your table and listen. Do not even listen, simply wait. Do not even wait, be quiet, still and solitary. The world will freely offer itself to you to be unmasked, it has no choice, it will roll in ecstasy at your fee.

By meditating on a regular basis you will become more relax and it will be easier for you to enter into this state of awareness with ease. The easier it becomes, the easier it will become for you to connect to the God's Rau. In time, you will also find as you continue with this practice that your patience and self – control will increase. For instance, if you are in the habit of getting angry at any little thing, this practice will help you to slow your response to become angry.

One of the great benefits of meditating is that you can ask for divine assistance by simply asking, "How can I achieve this goal while serving the greatest good?" You can also ask when in a bind, "What is the lesson I am supposed to learn from this situation?" or "How can I benefit from this?" You can even ask the question aloud and allow the answer to drift to your awareness.

The more you meditate the more you will learn with practice that the only way a person can annoy you is if you allow them to do so. This is because through meditation you will learn that you can control your own actions and reactions. One of the simplest ways to ensure that you remain calm and relaxed in the face of certain individuals is by meditating how you will react in a given situation. For instance, if you are in the habit of becoming annoyed whenever someone asks for a favor. If you want to change your reaction, when you meditate you would imagine the person asking for the favor, but instead of you becoming annoyed you imagine yourself being calm and relaxed. Repeat the process until you see the desired change in your behavior. This process is called in the shamanic tradition sowing dreams and it can be done to change most habitual reactionary behaviors. That is anything we are in accustomed to responding to a certain way. As always, when you finish meditating always say "Thank you" for the peace you receive from this practice.

Chapter 3:
Exploring the Three Aspects of Our Awareness

Understanding that God is everywhere (seen and unseen) and in everything means that God's Rau is beyond and deep within. We can therefore, access God's Rau anywhere but the simplest way to connect to God's Rau is by going deep within our being. When we go within, we connect or reconnect back to the Rau – the indestructible essence of God, which is how we acquire eternal love, self-control, freedom, health, prosperity, relief from fear and anxiety, personal fulfillment, wisdom, contentment and peace of mind, and much, much more that is commonly called spiritual enlightenment. Consequently, we are all programmed to reconnect back to the Rau. To help us to accomplish this task, we have nine parts our being that have been conveniently categorized into three divisions. These three divisions correspond indirectly to the three aspects of our mind: the ba (superconscious), sahu (subconscious) and ab (conscious).

The Ba: Our Divine Spark Within

God instilled within us all a divine spark that the Kamitic philosophers called the ba – the divine consciousness. The ba corresponds to what some call the superconscious, the higher self and the higher-division of our spirit also called the spark of God within. Our ba is directly connected to God's Rau, so it is able to implement changes because its tool of choice is divine energy. We all experienced God's Rau prior to being born, which is the reason we all have a strong desire to reconnect back to God. It is because of our ba, we all feel like we were created to do something spectacular in life even if we do not know what our purpose in life is.

The Ba and Our Ancestry

Our ba is the homing division of our being that pressures us to return back to God when things get hectic in the physical world, which is why the Kamitic philosophers described it as having a head of a human but the body of a hawk.

The main purpose of our ba is to help us to harmoniously create mental and physical experiences. In other words, the ba helps us create solutions by intuitively inspiring us with new and innovative ideas, which may come to us while reading a book, in a dream, while watching TV, praying, cooking, eating, painting, meditating, etc. For this reason, the ba is usually associated with our ancestors and/or some great patriarchal figure that was the first to connect to God and establish the bridge for future generations to follow. In many of the traditional African traditions, the ancestors are usually thought to be the first tribal clan leaders, whose true history has been lost but exist as mystical beings. In the Yoruba tradition, it is Obatala and the first tribal ancestors are called the orishas. In other spiritual traditions like Judaism, the patriarch was Abram who became Abraham and Moses, whom both had a close relationship with the Great Jehovah or I Am. In Christianity it was Jesus who opened the way for disenfranchised and disgruntled Jews and Gentiles, to connect with the Holy Ghost and so on. The Jewish and Christian writers all borrowed this concept from Kamitians philosophers who called the patriarchal figure in the Kamitic tradition Osar[9] and the first mystical ancestors are called the netcharu (guardian angels).

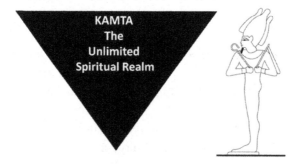

KAMTA
The
Unlimited
Spiritual Realm

Figure 6: Ruler of KAMTA

---

[9] Osar was inspired by the first dynastic king of Kamit Menes (Narmer), who is credited for unifying the kingdom.

38

Although anyone can talk to their ba, most people get a better understanding of their ba – the higher division of the spirit, when they personify it, which is why it is commonly called God by many in these contemporary times, but the ba is not the God. This is why the Kamitic thinkers personified it and called it Osar and early Christian writers referred to it as Jesus. Therefore, by listening and following our ba who speaks through the archetype Abraham, Moses, Jesus, Mohammed, Buddha or Osar, we are in essence returning to our original state of being and reconnecting back to the Divine, hence spiritual enlightenment.

The ba corresponds to KAMTA on the Maa Aankh, which was also the name for Upper Kamit. As a symbol of our awareness, it represents our Higher Spirit/Self and therefore our Highest Energy, which relates to Osar.

How We Become Disconnected from God

So that we are all clear, there is only one God, who is unimaginable, incomprehensible, and inconceivable, which is why we no one has been able to see the face of God. Like a blazing fire that we cannot physically touch, we can experience God's essence, spirit or power, which is called Rau. God's Rau is the divine essence that exists in everything. It is in esoteric terms the computer banks of eternal knowledge that can gives us eternal joy, eternal love, eternal peace, eternal patience, kindness, goodness, the gift of prophecy and the gift of healing, which are all attributes and virtues that we cannot obtain physically.

The Rau manifests itself within us as our ba, which all beings possess, because it gives everything that exist a purpose. Every thing that physically exists follows God's Divine plan, even human beings, but we get off the divine track because of our ego.

Most of us know that our ego is what disconnects us from the Divine but don't understand how and why. The reason is because so much has been written about spiritual enlightenment that the subject has become quite confusing. Presently the very mention of the term "spiritual" conjures up images of an old, frail bearded guru sitting on a mountaintop meditating in a lotus position, waiting for us to ask the deepest and most profound questions about life. For some of us, this image is so strong that we have fantasized that this cross-legged sitting man is floating on a cloud, because he has given up all of his material goods to become a world sage. In return they have acquired the secrets of the universe that allowed them to do some miraculous activities.

Let me reiterate what was stated earlier. Spiritual enlightenment is our original state of being, because we have reconnected back to the indestructible, unimaginable and pure essence of the Divine to bring about change beyond our physical control. These images that most of us have about spiritual enlightenment, along with the idea that spiritual enlightenment requires that you be poor, a bum, etc. are all beliefs and ideas created and maintained by our ego. In the future, we will see why our ego likes to throw these images up in our awareness, but for now. Every idea that you have that makes you feel as if you are disconnected from everyone around you, including God, are also false ideas (illusions) that come from your ego. This includes thoughts and ideas that you are stupid, you can't make it, you can only depend upon your self, you are too old, you are too young and so on.

Why does our ego give us all of these negative thoughts and ideas? Why does our ego make us believe that we can't trust anyone, that certain people are our enemies and that we are disconnected from God's Rau when it is everywhere and within us? Why is it so easy to accept that that we are created in the image of God and, that our family, friends, coworkers and peers are also created in the image of God. But, hard to remember that the annoying neighbor, the guy that cut you off in traffic, the drug pusher on the corner, the convicted rapist, the thief that burglarized the elders across the street home, are also made in the image of God? Why is it so easy to forget about our divinity?

The Sahu and Our Garment

The reason it is so easy to forget about our divinity is because when God created all the things in the universe. In order for every thing that was created to physically experience life. It needs a physical vessel that

40

would shield it from the elements and help it to instinctively survive. This physical vessel is what the Kamitic philosophers called the sahu – our physical body consciousness, which mimics our ba perfectly. The sahu from a physiological perspective it is our brain. It corresponds to the subconscious part of our being, thereby providing us with a physical body and all of the mental tools needed, like our memory, emotions and instincts, in order for us to physically survive.

The way the sahu functions, is that it helps us to learn about environment and other surroundings by storing memories in our body. The sahu ensures that our genetic memories are stored on the cellular level, which determines our sex, physical characteristics, etc. Learned memories are stored within our muscles, so when a certain event occurs like a fire. It triggers our muscles to react by fleeing the danger in order to avoid bodily harm. When something pleasant occurs our sahu triggers us to react by moving towards that which is pleasurable.

Everything that physically exists therefore has a ba – divine spark, divine consciousness or higher spirit, and a sahu – physical consciousness or lower spirit. This includes things such as plants and rocks, as well as animals, which explains why animals are able to exist and demonstrate a sign of intelligence.

The problem with the sahu is that it cannot distinguish between right or wrong, good or bad, etc. because it categorizes all of our memories according to how we feel. Good emotions are categorized as being good memories, whereas bad emotions are considered bad memories. But, we know that everything in life is not clear-cut and black and white. This is because everything that gives us pleasure is not necessarily good for us, just like everything that we find unappealing is not necessarily bad. Take for instance, sweets like chocolates chips cookies. If it were up to our sahu (if we like chocolate chips cookies) we would eat them continuously and receive no nutritional value for them. Let's jump to an even worst scenario, such as some foods that are harmful to some of us, and various substances leading to substance abuse. Do you get the picture?

So you see, the sahu is like the kid in all of us. When it does its job, it is great, but when put in a situation where we have to make a wise decision. It fails because this is not its purpose. Its purpose is to help us to survive by storing our memories so that we can learn from past and present experience. It primary reason for getting us to achieve anything is pleasure.

It is from our sahu that our ka (character/personality) is formed, which the Kamitic philosophers saw was obtained similar to the way we receive clothing, hence a garment. To understand this analogy, think about how when we are all born into this world, we are born as naked babes. Now imagine, after checking the vitals, the newborn is wrapped in some type of fabric to keep it warm. This is the first garment this child receives that it begins to associate with security, warmth and love. As the child grows older, the guardian of the child continues to clothed her or him in clothing that communicate security, love and warmth, but the child also provided clothing by extended family, the community, religious groups, peers, schools, society, etc. All of the programs that the child receives are like clothing for the child.

Imagine as the child continues to grow how now they are clothed in different attire for different events e.g. retire, when the parents go out to dinner, when visiting family and friends, etc. Next, when the child begins to attend school, they began to change their clothing according to their friends, the media and the environment. It doesn't take long for the child to learn that the attire they wear will either make them accepted or distanced them from their peers. Whatever choice that child makes, stays with them and will continue to influence the way they live for the remaining years on the planet.

So you see, some of us have been in hostile environments and are wearing survival garments to black tie events, while others are wearing three – piece suits to picnics. We are either underdress or overdressed for the occasion. Imagine showing up to a presidential dinner with camouflage pants, tourniquets and bandages on how those in attendance would react. They would most likely be alarmed. On the flip side, imagine wearing a three – piece suit to a summer picnic where everyone in attendance is in summer attire. This is why according to Kamitic philosophy, when problems arise in our life, instead of praying to God to remove the obstacles and give you what you desire. All you

42

have to do is simply change your attire. Sounds simple enough, right? But, there is a catch.

The Power of Our (Physical) Garment

We all have different ka–personalities/garments that we start wearing as soon as we are born, but we all don't wear the same thing. Our parents depending upon their likes and dislikes influence the type of garments we wear. In the infancy of our life, if we are boy we are dressed in blue outfits and if we are girls we wear pink outfits after birth, but as we grow older and began to interact with others. We began to wear different garments that either makes us accepted or rejected from our peers. This creates in our mind the belief that we are all separated and that some of us are more privilege than others. Because some of us have more garments than others. It also creates in our mind that we are what we possess, so the more garments – "things" – that we acquire the better off we are in life.

Do you see how we forget about our divinity? Our sahu is doing its job by providing us with a garment to shelter us from the elements and help us to survive, but at the same time. The more garments we wear, the more distant we become from our higher self because our garments convince us that we are what we wear, eat, whom we associate with and finally what we have physically acquired in our life. It gives us a false sense of who, we are because we begin to believe we are what we have and what we have accomplished.

Our garments also make us feel that we are separate from others. If someone is not wearing a garment similar to ours or more expensive, then we tend to believe that this individual is beneath us. We only respect those individuals whose garments are more expensive than ours only because we want the same type of garments that these individuals have. In separating us from others, we also tend to believe that we are disconnected from the things we want out of life and disconnected from God. This is because the garment hides the essence of God in all things and it prevents us from seeing it in others. Of course, all we have to do is simply change our garment and all of this would change. But, here lies the next problem.

43

If our garment is supposed to help us to live by providing us what we need to physically survive, but at the same time it prevents us from seeing our divinity and the divinity in others. How are we supposed to change the garment we are wearing and what are we supposed to change into?

Identifying Your (Physical) Garment

Have you ever dreamed of living on a tropical island and having a simple life? Have you ever wished you could go to a remote region of the world and just live with nature? What stops you from doing it?

If you mentioned money, your job, family, friends, or anything that physically exists, which you feel that if you didn't have you would not be happy. You have just listed all of the things that have convinced you that you need in order to be content. These are all of the things that have convinced you who you are but are concealing your divinity. All of these things that you identify with are different accessories to your garments. Please understand that I am not in any way saying that you do not need these things, because you do. You just don't need them to be happy. True joy cannot come from these things only from the Rau.

Although I am using the garment as a metaphor, I hope you can see that our garment is all of things that we have acquired and identify with. It is our clothes, cars, houses, accomplishments, degrees, jobs, careers, money, etc., which we believe makes us who we are and makes us treat others the way we do. They are the things given to you to help you to physically survive, but they will not bring you eternal peace or bliss. This is the reason you feel miserable when these things are gone, because your garment is your ego.

Our ego rules us 99.9% of the time because we identify with the things that have helped us to physically survive. In other words, most of our actions and behaviors are all based upon our egocentric impulses, such as what we will lose or gain based upon our actions. As a result, the reason we can't seem to resolve any of our problems is because the things we identify with the most is the probable cause of our dismay.

44

The Threads of Our (Physical) Garment

If our garment is our ego, then anger, anxiety, despair, false and excessive pride, frustration, laziness, pessimism, prejudice, rage, resentment, selfishness, worry and most of all, jealousy, are all of the threads woven to make our garment. These are emotional traits that drive our ego. It is our ego that is the driving force behind most of our actions and behaviors. It is what makes us fight others to convince them we are right, even at times when we are wrong. It compels us in an argument to want to get the last word. It prevents us from humbling ourselves in order to learn from others. It forces us to talk about our selves in order to impress others. It convinces us that if we work hard and long enough. We will obtain all that we want by ourselves.

Our ego is a 'work of art' and it convinces us that everything that we are doing is of our free will. A closer look however will reveal that most of our actions and behaviors are driven by one or more of the egocentric desires listed above. But, at the root of these desires is envy.

Envy[10] is an emotion of discontent and resentment aroused when an individual lacks a possession, qualities or achievement that another possesses, which means when someone is envious of another. They desire to have or possess something that another possesses. Now I must admit that like most people, I knew that it was wrong to envy another. It is one of the Christian tenets that I was taught in the church. So, when I looked at someone who is driving a luxury automobile. It didn't occur to me to steal the car from them, but what I didn't know. Is that when our ego desires the car or something similar to it, the ego will motivate us to work at trying to possess the same thing or something similar. Not only that, our ego does the same thing for everything that we have and everything that we want. This means that although, some of us may not see it, the reality is that we are

---

[10] Parrott, W. G., & Smith, R. H. (1993). *Distinguishing the experiences of envy and jealousy*. Journal of Personality and Social Psychology, 64, 906-920.

imprisoned by our ego, which compels us to try and outdo our family, friends, coworkers and colleagues. All because of envy.

This begs us to ask, where did the ego come from and how did we get these garments? The answer is that it comes from the early experiences we had in life and the things that we depended upon to help us to survive. If we keep in mind that our sahu, which corresponds to our subconscious, meaning everything that we learned – both the good and the bad, it is easy to see how that our ego evolved from all of our conditionings and early childhood influences. It is from these influences that a false image of who we are and supposed to be were created. This is why we identify with our family, friends, our education, degrees, how much money we have, our job, the clothes we wear, the car we drive, the house(s) we own, the people we associate with, our background, etc., which are all nothing but garments.

The Sahu and the Real Owner of Our (Physical) Garment

It is not that money, our clothes, cars; houses, etc. are evil, as some may claim. According to Kamtic thought, it is our identification with these things and the idea that it can bring us true joy and peace, other than God that is considered to be evil, hence an idol. To get a better understanding of the shadow aspect of our sahu, the Kamitic philosophers empowered it by personifying it, so that they could learn how to conquer it. Anger, anxiety, despair, false and excessive pride, frustration, laziness, pessimism, prejudice, rage, resentment, selfishness, worry and most of all, jealousy was all epitomized and called Set, the author of confusion, chaos, destruction, the lord of storms and war. Later he became known as Set-an, Satan, the Beast, Lucifer and the Devil.

Set, has been successful in deceiving all of us (our parents and elders included) because he is our ego, which is attached to our sahu. It should now make sense why we all don't have the same problems, because we each have our own personal devils.

46

For some of us it is a hard pill to swallow because we are still clinging on to the old deceptions. That the devil is some impish red skinned man running around on hooved legs with a pitchfork. The truth of the matter is that the devil is real and he exists inside you and me. He is in all of us and everyone will have to fight him someday like Jesus did when the deceiver tempted him in the Judean desert. If you are having a difficult time accepting that Set is inside you, it is because he has really deceived you. The great news is that the sooner we accept this, the easier it will be for us to understand the great writings of the various spiritual masters[11], as well as get on with the rest of our life.

When you see through Set's lies. It explains why when people act as animals and do evil. They seem to go into a fit of rage and become violent, because these are all traits from the ego. It makes sense why people lie and knowing doing wrong, because the ego is selfish and pessimistic. It even explains why some of the people we have chosen to represent us and upholds the law; commit some of the most atrocious and heinous crimes despite their good behavior, affluence, backgrounds, education, and reputations. Clearly, they are all ego driven, because Set – the devil is our ego and he is the ruler of TASETT, which as I am sure you can see now is the perfect symbol for our Lower Self and Lower Consciousness.

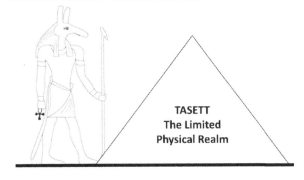

TASETT
The Limited
Physical Realm

[11] Logically it makes no sense as to why the devil would tempt God knowing that the odds are clearly against him. When it is accepted that Jesus was not God incarnate but an ordinary human being like you in me. It makes sense why the devil tempted Jesus and why Jesus was victorious over his enemy.

Figure 7: Ruler of TASETT

The Ab and the Human Soul

But we were not created to be animals. God has enough animals running around in the forests and the seas. God created Man and Woman, because God wanted a vessel in order to express Himself through. God wanted to create, draw, paint, build, etc. in order to demonstrate His/Her[12] ability. The thing is that our ba (the higher division of our spirit) or Osar will not intervene in our life unless asked to do so. This is why we as human beings were created and given a human soul and self-awareness called the ab or ab - soul.

The ab –soul is what gives human beings the ability to choose and make decisions, unlike animals that must follow their instincts or the sahu division of their being. Our ab corresponds to our conscious mind and also our determination and will. For this reason, the ab – soul was called the spiritual heart. By referring to the ab – soul as our spiritual heart, the analogy is simple; whatever is inside a man or woman's heart is what controls his and her actions. Therefore, if a man or woman has a lustful heart they will be lustful in their actions and behaviors. At the same time, if a man or woman had a strong heart, it indicated that this individual would have a strong disposition, which is why we continue to say to this day, that people who are courageous, honorable, etc. have "heart."

The ab also corresponded to an individual's conscience indicating that when an individual had done ill, they had a guilty conscience because their ab was heavy and weighed down by sin. Since, the ba divinely inspires us but our sahu encourages us based upon the right or wrong beliefs, ideas and memories we have acquired from others while living. Sinful acts and behaviors come from the sahu division of our being, which means to rid one's self of sin (anxiety, fear, guilt, worrisome, anger, lust, etc. – all animalistic behaviors) they need to purify and purge it from their ab – soul. In other words, all of the

---

[12] God is essentially androgynous or genderless, meaning God is technically an It or Being.

48

emotions that prevent us from achieving what we want out of life and hold us back from reconnecting to God, so that we may have true peace, eternal happiness, and prosperity, require that develop a strong heart, determination and will or ab – soul.

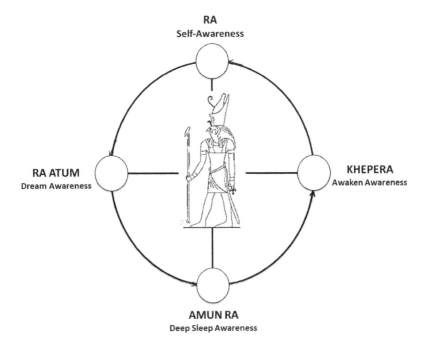

Figure 8: Ruler of the Sun

The Kamitic philosophers understanding that the ab – soul is the only aspect of our being that separates us from animals and all of the other living beings. It is also the only aspect of our being that we can truly control, thereby reflecting our true identity, divinity, and giving us authority and the power to control our own lives; personified the ab – soul by identifying it as the hawk masked man called Hru (Greek Horus, the son of Osar) and symbolizing it celestially as the sun to represent our free will and ever changing consciousness.

When we compare this to the Maa Aankh, we see that Khepera also corresponds to our awaken awareness. Ra represents for most of us our normal state of consciousness where one is able to identify various events occurring in their environment, which is also referred to as self-awareness. Ra Atum symbolized our loss of conscious awareness, which

49

occurs when we retire and go to sleep. This state of awareness is sometimes called the dream state of awareness, while Amun Ra corresponds to our deep sleep awareness where one has the ability to be totally objective, which is uninfluenced by one's emotions or particular prejudices.

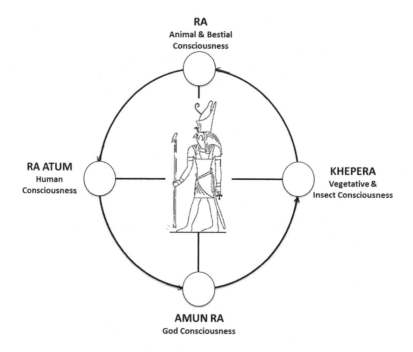

Figure 9: Evolution of Divine Consciousness

Metaphorically speaking it can be said that our conscious evolves from Khepera (vegetative and insect consciousness) to Ra (animalistic and bestial consciousness), then to Ra Atum (human consciousness) and, finally to Amun Ra (god consciousness).

What this means is that because our ab-soul is essentially free, we are not obligated to do anything. We have complete authority over our lives and therefore whatever we perceive in our mind, will become a physical reality in our life. We simply need to learn how to strengthen our will[13] in order to tap into our divinity. When our ab – soul and will

---

[13] This is the reason the hawk is used to symbolize the ab – soul because it is a trainable predatory animal.

is not strong, our awareness on the evolutionary cycle is low. Therefore, the stronger our ab – soul and will, the closer we come to the Divine and obtaining a God Consciousness.

The Purpose of the (Physical) Garment

When we look at life from this perspective it indicates that the purpose of the garment and all of the other obstacles that we have in our life, is basically to help us to develop our ab – soul. The garment that our sahu provides us with basically creates all of the adversities that we will have in life. It is because of our garment we fall, but if we never fell, we would never know how to rise and stand up. If we never learned how to crawl, we would never learn how to walk. If we never experienced any problem or tribulation, we would not know how to cope and deal with it. Our garments are basically all of the lessons wrapped up in one package to make our life miserable, in order to motivate us to develop our will and become godlike.

Now, you know why your annoying neighbor exists, so that you can learn to tolerate others. It is the reason you were given a child that likes to get into things, so that you can develop patience. It is why you keep getting into oppressive relationships, so that you can learn to conquer fear and stand up for yourself. It is the reason why you were put in a position to lead, so that you can learn humility and how to listen. Anything and everything that gets on your nerves was put there so that you can learn how to remove this impurity from your soul.

Our garment, which is based upon what we physically see, translates what emanates from our ab – soul into the physical world. In other words, whatever we focus our ab – soul awareness upon is what manifests itself in our physical life. Hence, if you believe you are stupid, then you will be put in situations where people will treat you as such. If you believe you are intelligent and capable of achieving anything, then you will be put in situations that will allow you to express your intelligence. It is all about determining what you want out of life and physically working to achieve it. This means that most of our disappointments and failures are simply due to us not having a pure and strong ab – soul.

51

Therefore, in order to accomplish any objective (spiritual or mundane) as well as purify one's ab – soul of sin (the things of the flesh). What we have to learn to do is use our garments (learning experiences, education, money, skills, talents, resources, etc.) as a tool and not allow our garment(s) to control and decide who and what we are. The reason is because if we do not, we run the risk of having our destructive beliefs, more specifically our fears that reside within our sahu, prevent us from becoming who we were meant to be.

For instance, it is the fear that we will be homeless or lose our security that prevents us from starting a business or learning how to invest. It is the fear that we will be hurt that prevents us from pursuing a meaningful relationship. It is the fear of what others might say about us that prevents us from sharing our skills and talents with those who could benefit from it. Unfortunately, by giving into our fears we inadvertently create the physical reality we were trying to prevent.

This is because as we have read, it is our ba that aligns us with the Divine, but the sahu puts us in the challenging situation to purify our ab – soul. When we choose the higher road by ignoring our fear we are put on the correct path for greatness. This means that each time we give into our ego, it sets us back from missing an opportunity. We are all one to two steps away from meeting that special someone, landing that dream job, stepping on the path to fulfill our destiny, etc. but it can only be achieve by overcoming our fear encouraged by Set.

This is where spiritual development comes into the picture, because in order to accomplish this we have to learn self – control and self – discipline. Self-control and self – discipline is symbolized by the

Pschent crown; thereby indicating one's kingdom KAMTA and TASETT are united within.

Exercise 3:
How to Begin to Cleanse the Soul

One way to begin purifying your ab - soul is by temporarily disconnecting it from our sahu or "metaphorically" taking off your garments and returning to Nature. Since Nature doesn't wear garments and is natural, original, direct, primal and ancient. Nature doesn't have any dichotomies such as good and bad, right or wrong, etc. In nature, there is just our soul and it strips away all of our garments. The theory is that by denying our sahu certain things. We can purify our ab – soul of the egotistical aspects like excessive pride, anger, despair, etc. and return to our more natural state of being.

This is the original idea behind such ascetic practices as taking a vow of poverty, consuming only raw (not cooked) foods, converting to vegetarianism, etc. but when taken to the extreme. These practices become dogmatic, imbalanced and unnatural because they are denying the body of essential nutrients that it needs, not to mention other problems that may be caused due to this decision. This is similar to using only the right side of the body and never using the left. An example of such is the erroneous belief that in order to connect to the Divine or "more spiritual" you have to be a vegetarian, which is simply not true because we are never disconnected from God. We may not be attuned to God because of our state of awareness, but we are always connected to God. So unless we are using vegetarianism as a means of detoxifying the body, it is not necessary for our spiritual development[14]. This is why it is very important that you understand that ascetic practices should only be done temporarily and not permanently, so as to not endanger one's physical and mental health.

The easiest and safest way however to purge our ab – soul of impurities is by fasting, which when done correctly. Is one of the best spiritual disciplines that can helps strip us of the garments of the sahu

---

[14] If you are considering vegetarianism as a lifelong practice, be sure to see a qualified health professional that will help design a dietary plan, so that you can be sure to get all the necessary nutrients that your body needs.

and get us back to the original state of our being. This discipline was used by shamans all over the world to help them to prepare spiritually before undertaken a serious task. It is also used in most major religions.

Fasting had a very profound and rich meaning in the early African Americans community because they combined their traditional understandings of the practice with Christianity. In Christianity it was taught that after Jesus was baptized he went on a 40 day fast, thus meaning that the purpose of baptism was to purify oneself of sin but early African Americans interpreted this slightly different.

Sin or illness, problems with the law, obstacles, tribulations, gross humiliation, etc. they believed were contracted throughout life because of gross impurities (erroneous belief, bad thoughts, etc.) that our (ab) soul picked up as we walked through this life, which resulting in the setting of one's personal sun (anguish, misery, problems, trouble, etc.). Since the BaKongo[15] culture believed that the spiritual world was upside down and connected to the physical world by a watery barrier called kalunga line or nyun (see figure 1 & 2) in Kamitic language (symbolized as the horizontal line between Kala - birth and Luvemba - death). In order to be renewed or born again (change of consciousness and way of life), they not only had to be ritualistically cleaned but they also had to fast. As a result, it was customary that whenever someone suffered from a condition or serious problem. To take a ritual bath to remove the impurity and fast to be renewed or born again like the rising sun, so that whatever was wreaking havoc in their life would be removed.

This cultural approach created positive change because it combined praying, ritual bathing and fasting together. It worked because it follows the principle that whatever the attention is focused on, that is where the energy goes. As a result, one's ab – soul awareness moves from an extroverted state to an introverted state of awareness where they may have visions, out of body and other mystical experiences.

---

[15] BaKongo means "People of the Kongo."

Although there are number of pretty smelling and beautiful colored baths waters and salts that can be obtained from spiritual supply stores. Most of these products were not made by spiritually minded individuals but instead machines. A lot of them do not even contain natural ingredients. Again, most of the time, the early spiritual workers used basic and easy to find ingredients, many of which could be found right around one's own home. Below is a listing of common conditions and spiritual baths that can be taken.

Purpose	Herb	Incense & Bathe With	Natural Food Coloring
Attraction	Parsley, Cilantro	Cinnamon / Honey	Yellow
Courage	Red Pepper	Frankincense/ Pumice Soap or Stones	Red
Health	Peppermint	Myrrh/ White Sage	Green
Purification	Anise	Coconut/Salt	Blue
Protection	Wintergreen	Allspice/ Seashells	Blue
Power	Mustard Seeds	Dragon's Blood/Pine Needles	Red & Blue
Wealth	Bayberry	Honeysuckle/ Money	Green

Generally the bath was taken for seven or nine days, or for however long the fast would last. The herbs were prepared into a tea and then poured into the bath water. To activate, say a prayer over the water to bless it with the intended purpose. While sitting in the bath a prayer of your own words can be said or you can read the corresponding Psalms while contemplating on your purpose. Be sure after taking the bath that you clean the tub and remove the debris so that it does not come in contact with others. These baths can be taken while burning a candle associated with the bath color or if this is not possible, a white candle, but this is not necessary.

One can fast from more than food, such as a solid food fast. In fact, it is a common practice that while fasting to abstain from other activities that your sahu enjoys such as watching television, sex, listening to certain types of music and so on. There are three types of fasts that are commonly done according to one's capabilities and needs. They are:

1. Sunrise to Sunset Fast – where one fasts from sun up to sundown. This is also called the "Six to six" fast.
2. The Three Days Fast – where one fasts only during the day for three days.
3. The Seven Day (or Week) Fast – which is where one fasts for an entire week and does not eat anything during the day.

There are additional fasts that are done such as fasting for seven days and nights where one does not eat or drink. This in my opinion is border lining on asceticism. Anyone that fasts beyond the Seven Day Fast should be very cautious for reasons stated above. If you are considering going beyond the Seven Day Fast, I strongly recommend that you seek the advice of a licensed health professional to ensure that you are in an optimal state of health to do so.

Chapter 4:
How to Defeat the Enemy

It should be clear by now that there is a war going on and the war is between our higher and lower self. This war has been going on forever and the devil Set is winning because he has tricked us all into believing that he did not exist. So, the question is how do we defeat our enemy within?

Well, there's an old Cherokee legend that I once heard. In the story the grandfather is telling his grandson about life. The grandfather says that he feels like there are two wolves fighting inside of his heart. One wolf the grandfather said is angry, arrogant, envious, vengeful, violent and full of self-pity, false pride and sorrow. The other wolf is compassionate, honorable, loving, and full of joy, hope, humility, faith and peace. The grandson curiously asked, "Which one will win?" and the grandfather answered him saying, "The one I feed." In other words, it is the one that we give the most attention to.

Just about every culture that has walked the earth has expressed in one way or another, the same confusion that occurs within our being between our higher and lower self. This internal conflict that has been allegorized as a battle between God and the devil, as you can see literally has nothing to do with God per se. It is all about us learning how to conquer and defeat our lower self. It is the inability to conquer our lower self that prevents God from manifesting miracles in our life. This is why the Kamitic philosophers who were very knowledgeable about the human psyche, distinctly associated the lower spirit of our being with Set, so that people didn't get it twisted and think that the devil is just an entity outside of our awareness.

When we get a clear understanding what our higher and lower self are, we see that basically our Set motivates us to act and behave like petty, little spoiled children ruled by our emotions of anger, guilt, fear, etc. It is Osar who encourages us instead to choose the higher road by resisting the habit to react, thus avoiding confrontation with others, by being proactive and looking for a solution that would be best for all the parties involved. Set as you can see is all about our selfish desires, while

Osar is concerned about the needs of all. Another way of looking at it is that Set is solely pro self, while Osar is pro-family, community, etc. Defeating Set is possible, but it takes a lot work and requires that we really understand how our sahu functions.

Exploring the Sahu Further

The reason it is so difficult to defeat our ego – the devil or Set, is because as mention earlier when it comes to anything spiritual. He throws up images of an old man meditating on a remote mountaintop because he is totally against change. Since, Set dwells within our sahu, he knows all of our likes and dislikes and uses whatever image or illusion he can find in our past or in the present. To discourage us from doing what we want. This means that if you are having problems. If you review the problems, you will find most likely that it is usually because of an old memory that you are dwelling upon. This is because Set knows what you want, even when you try to deny it from yourself. If you are having relationship problems in your marriage, Set will knowingly push the both of you to the breaking point and make the easy route to divorce seem more appealing because it is less painful, then coming together and working things out like responsible adults. Set seeks the easy route of escape because remember the sahu's main incentive for doing things is pleasure. Change is not always pleasurable, which is why Set is a pleasure hog always motivating us to take the easy way out and mimic what others have done in our past.

In fact, when put in a situation where we have to make a decision, our Set will convince us to take the less painful route, especially if we do not have any good reason for doing otherwise. For instance, if we are working at a job that we do not like, and the only reason we are there is because we need the money. Our Set will look around find a way for us to leave by influencing us to get into an altercation or maybe causing us to become ill in some way. From Set's perspective, it is better to be sick or to be fired then to put up with an agonizing supervisor that takes advantage, misuses and disrespects us. It is easy to see when we personify the lower self as Set, the motivation behind negative actions and behavior.

Fortunately, things aren't as bleak as they may seem. Thankfully, the Kamitic philosophers understanding the dilemma we were in discovered thousands of years ago. That the way to defeat the devil is by living one's life based upon the dynamics of importance. In other words, people will knowingly bite down and bear the pain, so long as they keep in mind, the end result or goal of what they are doing is considered more important, and therefore more pleasurable. Olympic hopefuls for instance will train every day for long hours because want they want to win the gold medal, and want the fame and prestige that comes along with winning. Serious minded college students will study all hours of the night, get tutoring and abstain from various extracurricular activities, in order to get their degree. Simply put the Kamitians discovered that the gain has to be exponentially greater than the pain. If there is no benefit to staying in a relationship with someone, Set will definitely give you a reason based upon your past or the present to get out.

Since the sahu (the lower division of our spirit), which cannot distinguish between the past, present or future, is responsible for our physical body consciousness, and it stores. All of our genetic memories on the cellular level and learned memories in our muscles which, when stimulated by a particular event will either cause our body to become relaxed or tensed depending upon the memory we dwell upon. That in turn will produce endorphins if we dwell upon good memories or toxins if we dwell upon the negative ones. The indirect way to control our emotions and change our life is by creating new memories and focusing on them, similar to the practice that was done in Exercise 2.

When we choose to consciously create new memories using our ab – soul, since the main function of our ba (the higher division of our spirit) is to create new mental and physical experiences, our sahu memorizes the new memory because it cannot distinguish between the past, present or future or what is real and not real. While our ba makes the memory a reality and improves upon our goal by inspiring us with new and innovative ideas, because it is all about creating harmony. Because the ba is connected to everything, these inspiring ideas will come to us intuitively. They may appear in our awareness while reading a book, in a dream, while watching TV, praying, cooking, eating, painting, meditating, etc. Said another way, by focusing our will on what we want, our Set is tricked into serving our Osar and helping us to achieve our goal, which is allegorized in the *Story of Osar*.

The Story of Osar

Although it is a great story that has inspired timeless classics like Shakespeare's *Hamlet* and new classics like *The Lion King* don't be fooled into thinking that this is just a story about right over might. The *Story of Osar* can be and has been interpreted in many ways, but originally. It was like the Old Testament to the Jewish people and the New Testament to the Christians because it is a metaphoric code about the nature of our being. There are numerous versions of the story but they all have the same ending. When compared to the maa aankh you will get a better understanding of the *story*, the Kamitic culture and how it relates to your life.

In the story, Osar (symbolizing our ba) the ruler of the southern region, had dreamt of uniting his war torn country together[16], so he traveled the land teaching his people a set of laws to resolve their differences. After learning the science of agriculture from his devoted wife Oset, he taught the people how to cultivate the land, which made everyone in the region prosperous. As the teachings of Osar spread like wildfire, almost overnight Osar became a beloved ruler. He had accomplished his goal and everyone was grateful for him except for his youngest brother Set.

Set (the antagonist of the story symbolizing our ego) kills his eldest brother Osar (our ba) and usurps the throne (our life). In the story, as Set's spreads terror throughout the land, no one opposes him out of fear, which is an allusion about denial and how people choose not to take responsibility for the ill in the world, because they didn't do it. But, Osar's devoted wife Oset (the soul's our desire for positive change), refused to give into Set's terror. So she immediately put on her

---

[16] This obviously is an allegory that can be used to symbolize a host of concepts. In this passage it symbolizes the disunity between KAMTA and TASETT.

mourning clothes and went in search of the body of Osar. With the help of Npu (the spirit that opens the way), after Oset found the body of Osar she magically conceived and gave birth to Hru (our soul's will and determination to change). But, Set had managed to find the body of Osar and he hacked it up into 14 pieces. Later Oset along with Npu, her sister Nebhet (the ex-wife of Set) went in search for the body of Osar again. Every time they found a piece of the body, they built a shrine in its place, which helped to revive the memory of Osar. When all of the body parts had been recovered they along with Djahuti (Osar's wise vizier), mummified the body of Osar, gave him a proper burial and hid his body so that Set could never destroy it again. This of course, is a code explaining why our higher spirit is so distant from our lower spirit – ego.

When Hru comes of age he received instructions in a dream from Osar to avenge his father. So, the young prince raises an army to challenge Set for the throne. One of the allies who fight with Hru against Set's tyranny is Hruaakhuti also known as Hru-Behutet or Hru the Elder, which is an older brother of Set, but after several battles. Hru is defeated by Set because Set has gouged his eye out (an allusion about the devil's lies and illusions). After meeting Djahuti, Osar's wise vizier and friend, who repaired Hru's eye (an allusion indicating that he showed Hru how to see through Set's deception), Hru was able to defeat Set on the battlefield. But victory was not his yet, because Set had challenged Hru in court for the throne. For days (some say months and years) the tribunal that met to determine Hru's fate deliberated, because some favored the young prince but many out of fear sided with Set. Then through magical means, Osar was allowed to speak on Hru's behalf (alluding to the power of resistance against the weapons of Set (these weapons are listed in the next section). Shortly after, through a turn of events, the young prince was declared the victor by the tribunal. He was awarded the white and red Pschent crown, while Set was sentenced to propel the boat of Osar. This is a reference to the creative intelligence of the sahu being used to assist us in achieving our will.

What Does It All Mean?

There are many interpretations that can be drawn from the story but in regards to fighting for our higher self. We see that it is an imbalance either way when we are polarized in KAMTA or TASETT. The story therefore implies that we are all Hru. We are all fighting Set for control of our lives. Our enemies are not our real enemy. Our real enemy is Set who manifests himself in all of us. When we see people doing ill, it is not because they are evil incarnate. It is because they have given into their Set. This is the time when they need the most help to change their consciousness. Please understand that I am not saying that when someone commits a crime that they should not be punished. Not at all, everyone has to learn the consequences of their actions. What I am saying is that a valiant effort should be made to uncover why the individual committed the crime to avoid similar crimes from being committed.

This is very important to understand because by focusing on the effects and not the cause. We fail to restore and resurrect all that Osar has created in our life. Life did not use to be so horrific. The reason it has become so bad is because our society each and every day continues to give into Set. Take for instance, the war on drugs. Billions of dollars have been spent on preventing drugs from entering into the United States alone. Yet drugs are still somehow making their way into our communities. Is the war on drugs working? Not according to the statistics and violent crimes report and the reason in my opinion is because. The primary cause is not being addressed.

We blame drug cartels for shipping drugs into our communities but the fact is that if there were no consumer, the seller would go out of business. The same can be said about every other addictive and destructive influence in our society including explicit lyrics and the degradation of women in music. The reason this type of music continues to be produced is because women (in general) and men have not taken a stance against it. If people simply stop buying it, it would force the record producing companies to change their view and thereby create a change in consciousness. Understand that I am not in any way condoning these negative activities but the truth of the matter is that unless awareness is raised. We can expect to keep fighting the wrong fight by focusing on the problem and not the solution.

This is what happens whenever we try to resolve a problem by relying upon our sahu. It is like trying to cut the head off the Greek hydra monster and once one head falls, two more grow in its place. The reason our sahu creates more problems then it solves is because we have to remember it derives all that it knows from our limited physical experience. If it never learned how to know how to resolve a problem efficiently, the easiest solution is to encourage us to shift blame upon someone or something else for our failures. When really all we need to do is take responsibility for our self and allow our intuition from our ba to be our guide.

Heaven & Hell Is a State Of Mind

Now I want you to pay very close attention to this, because following your ba or listening to your Osar does not mean. That if you intuit and try to resolve a problem that you have no knowledge about, that a solution will suddenly appear. For instance, if you have never been to medical school did your residency and never practiced medicine. You are not going to intuitively receive information about how to conduct an open-heart surgery because there is no physical outlet for your spiritual current. Even if you did receive such information you would not know what to do with it.

This is a clear sign that you are either being influenced by Set or you have encountered Set, because you shouldn't have to struggle and force anything approved by the Divine to happen. Note, I didn't say work hard, but struggle. The difference is when you struggle and try to force something to occur in your life. It is like trying to make someone love you, that does not have any interest in you at all. This also corresponds to acting, living and behaving from your sahu and listening to your Set. When this occurs you function from a very low frequency, which causes you to become anxious, angry, fretful, depressed, worried, etc. because you ego is driving or influencing your ab – soul. This is the reason TASETT is symbolized as an upward pointing triangle to remind us that everything that we physically see, due to our ab – soul being extroverted, is an allusion created by Set.

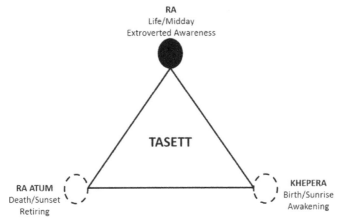

Figure 10: The Mental State of Hell

When we are being influenced by Set, we feel an elevated blood pressure and the flow of adrenaline because these are all signs of a heighted beta state of awareness. TASETT points towards Ra, which represents midday – the hottest time of the day, physiologically marked by anxiety, agitation, quickness in thoughts, the desire to act violently, etc. At this position, we are basically in a **<u>mental state of hell</u>** and this is why when people are totally controlled by their Set they commit heinous crimes.

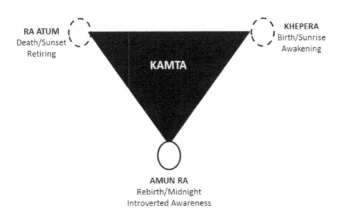

Figure 11: The Mental State of Heaven

There is a saying that "with every vision comes provisions," meaning that when you get the insight to do something. You will have all the necessary supplies to make it happen, which is why KAMTA is symbolized as downward pointing triangle pointing towards Amun Ra, which symbolizes the cool, collective and highest level of awareness. It is a reminder that when we introvert our awareness and rely upon our ba – the indwelling intelligence or our Osar. All of our needs will be taken care of. KAMTA we must remember is unlimited and we know that we have encountered our Osar when we feel a deep state of peace, relaxation and resolve, along with the desire to be diplomatic, which is basically a **mental state of heaven.**

It can therefore be concluded that the only way to ascend to heaven, you have to be at least familiar with it in mind[17].

Recognizing Who's Talking to You

This means that we need to recognize who is talking to us. To begin your quest in reclaiming your heritage, start by recognizing that Set being the youngest between him and Osar, is the one that sends clear and loud thoughts urging us to react. Usually his solutions are logical but they are too rational. For instance, as I had mentioned before, if we established our dietary plan based upon Set. It would have us eat cookies; cakes and ice cream all of the time because it knows that our sahu likes these deserts. Even though these deserts do not provide our body with the nourishment we need. This is what it meant by being too logical, Set tries to get us to justify our reactions using our likes and dislikes.

Osar, on the other hand, being more mature and resolute has a very distant voice that speaks from deep within. When Osar speaks (if he speaks at all) it usually comes as flash of insight, an intuitive thought, a vision or a message in our dreams. Osar's messages usually are focused on getting us stop in our forward movement, calm down, relax and look for a practical, yet positive solution. The secret to beating Set is to simply not give into him and go to his level. Set is very pleased when you focus on the problem because he knows that this is not the root. When we focus on the problem we are only focusing upon what

---

[17] This is the meaning behind ghosts not wanting to go into the Light out of fear.

66

we can physically see, which is why the problem he created will return. If we focus on the solution, the problem will reveal itself and then you're able to make the necessary corrections.

I am a witness of this because I used to get a skin rash out of the blue. It just came out of nowhere, all of a sudden. When it happened the first few times, I would put some ointment on and it would go away, but after it had occurred several times. I decided to go to the doctor. After doing some tests. The doctors found nothing wrong, but the rash would continue to come back up. Then one day, I had the strangest idea to ask my body why it was breaking out. Almost instantaneously, what came to mind was an image of me expressing my disgust for a particular individual. When I didn't want to be around a certain individual. I would work myself up by talking about how bad this individual was, how they got on my nerve and made me sick, etc., etc. It came to me that my sahu responded by creating an illness so that I didn't have to meet this individual. Its logic was that it is better to have an illness then it was to meet with this individual. So voila, it sent Set the plan and he went to work.

In order to recover from the illness, I apologized to my sahu, so that I wouldn't do it again and asked what I did not like about this individual. I discovered in the process that the individual stressed me out, so I imagined being in perfect health. Then I repeated before I went to bed and when I awoke, "Thank you for perfect health." During my leisure time, I stated "Thank you for perfect health" all while imagining myself participating in activities that as a healthy individual I would enjoy doing. When I was around the individual that got me stressed. I stop letting myself get stressed by them. When they did something annoying I just ignored it. In the end, it took some work but I stopped having skin eruptions and the individual that use to stress me out. I didn't allow myself to become stressed anymore.

Exercise 4:
How to Recognize Divine Signs

Now that you have learned how to recognize the Rau in the first
exercise and have begun to purify your ab – soul in the second exercise
by fasting, you need to learn how to distinguish between your feeling
and your thoughts. When you hear the terms "go within" or "go with
your gut," it refers to quieting the chatter of the mind in order to focus
on an issue and see how it makes you feel.

Many people think that their feelings and emotions are the same
thing, but they are not. Emotions for the most part are instinctive
reactions to situations causing you to e-mote or react. Emotions can be
triggered by a thought, a memory or some situation and they are long-
term. Your feelings on the other hand are triggered by external events
and are short term. Your emotions are internalized whereas your
feelings are triggered by external factors. For instance, anger,
happiness, sorrow, disgust, fear, worry, anxiety, peace, tranquility are
all emotions that can last for a long period of time. While hunger,
hunger, thirst, itching, funny, etc. are all feelings, which only last for a
short period of time. By learning the difference between the two it is
possible to discern the truth and best course of action to take when
faced with a difficult situation.

To begin this exercise, you need to get your journal. Next, sit
quietly, relax and clear your mind by not thinking about anything.
Simply allow all the thoughts to pass through your awareness as you
had done in exercise one. Just relax and be quiet. When you are totally
relaxed and at peace, tell yourself a true statement like, "My name is
(fill in your name)." After you make the statement notice how you feel
afterwards and how the statement resonates with your being. Describe
how you felt when you told the truth to yourself in your journal.

When you are finish, make a false statement like "My name is
(Make up a name)," and again notice how the lie makes you feel and
how it resonates with your being. Again write how a falsehood makes
you feel in your journal.

What you have just done is determined how truth and falsehood resonates with you. Notice how in which direction your eyes turn and if you feel a strong sensation in your gut or not. Some people when they tell the truth they feel a sense of calm and peace overcome them. Others have been known to get goose pimples. While some may feel as if their awareness is heightened and they are feel lively. When they tell a lie, their heart may races or they feel a sudden fear overcome them. Whatever you feel, take note of it and know that your feelings are different from others because we are all unique. If you did not feel a difference, don't get disheartened. You just need to keep practicing until you do.

Figure 12: The Red Flag of Set

Now, once you have learned how to discern how the truth and untruth feels. You can use this technique to determine how people, places and things will affect you. For instance, when get an untruth feeling from something, someone or a place you visit, then you know it is a red flag being raised warning of you to be cautious, because of approaching danger. The red flag corresponds to the Ra moment on the maa aankh cosmogram, which symbolizes approaching the Western wind, hence Ra Atum – the moment on the maa aankh that corresponds to death, serious change, etc. in TASETT.

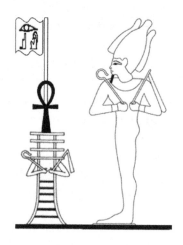

Figure 13: The White Flag of Osar

Whenever you get the truth feeling, envision your Osar raising a white flag. The white flag corresponds to the Amun Ra moment on the maa aankh cosmogram signifying the flag is being raised in KAMTA. It indicates that you are approaching the Khepera moment on the maa aankh – that corresponds to the birth of something new and spectacular.

By paying attention to your truth signs you can also discern if an activity is beneficial or harmful to you. Certain activities will cause your red flag to go up more quickly than others, but note that the longer your red flag stays raised. The more damage it has the potential of causing you, your kingdom. For instance, certain foods and drinks may cause your flag to go up. If you have impressed this image upon your sahu strong enough, it can signal to you when you have reached your limit to prevent you from overeating and drinking. Obviously it is best to keep the white flag raised and stay within this region.

You can also use this technique to determine when Set is driving you to do something out of fear, worry, etc. or if you are being inspired by your Osar. We live in a society that

This exercise is helpful in determining when you are receiving an omen or if it is just wishful thinking you are experiencing. If your

70

truth signs appear then you will know that the omen you experienced is not coincidence.

I have used this technique also to help me to distinguish when I am being inspired by my Osar or driven by my Set. For instance, we have all heard the proverb, "do unto others as you would have them do unto you." To me this doesn't just mean treating others with respect but also implies doing what I would for others, as I would do for myself. This is because a lot of times we do things in order to gain others approval. For those who don't know a couple of the hobbies that I picked up doing my recovery was doing artwork and cooking.

I noticed that when I cook or do artwork to gain another's approval, it doesn't come out right. If I am cooking trying to impress someone, the seasoning comes out all wrong. If it is artwork, they tend not to like it, because I am doing it for the wrong reason. I should only be concerned with getting one individual's approval and that is the God within me. When I change perspective and cook or do artwork as if I was in other's people's shoes. Everything tends to work out for the best. Instead of my trying to please everyone's palette for instance, I cook imagining how I would want certain foods to taste. I do artwork from the perspective of would I hang this piece on my wall, etc. My Set flag rises whenever I am doing something strictly for the money. When I doing something to benefit all, that's when my Osar flag, rises.

The technique is important because it helps us to see when and how the Divine communicates to us. When you are able to recognize the Divine signs and the signatures of the netcharu. You will notice that when you are rushing to work and get behind a white car with an elderly person driving. Instead of seeing it as an old person that can't drive, you may be inclined to recognize that it is Osar warning you to slow down and be patient. This is the type of relationship you will develop with your aakhu (ancestors) and netcharu (guardian spirits) once you begin to see how they manifest themselves in your life.

Chapter 5:
The Three Paths to Ultimate Power

By now, I hope that you see the reason for this philosophy is to teach you about your true Self and help you to conquer your real enemy – your lower spirit, with the help of your higher spirit. This is and has always been the only objective behind religion, but it often gets muddled because of dogmatic beliefs and practices. This is why you do not need to belong to any particular religion in order to implement the maa aankh into your life. If you are a Christian and you see beyond the lies of the devil, it is easy to see that the God in you is your ba, which if you prefer can call Jesus. It will make your spiritual growth and progress so much better and stronger, because you will be able to see how the devil attacks you and how you can defend, attack and claim victory.

The second reason for sharing this philosophy is to get you to see that if you don't conquer your Set. You will constantly live your life according to the whims of your ego, which means every little thing that happens you will react to in the most immature and horrible manner. If you are always reacting to life, you will always be the effect, or the tail. The enemy will always know how to get you to do his bidding because he knows what buttons to push. Remember, Set dwells in our sahu, so he knows your strengths and weaknesses or likes and dislikes. Now, this all about to change, because now you know that the only way to defeat him, is to stop reacting to the whims of your ego. As soon as you stop doing this, you will get the devil off your neck and instead of being the slave, you will become the master. This is when you will become the cause and began creating change in all areas of your life.

Finally, when you cease reacting to every little thing that happens to you and start becoming the cause. You would have encountered the third reason for this philosophy. You will understand that you didn't come to this realm to be good. You came to this physical realm to learn how to create and cause events to occur. You were born to overcome the destructive beliefs and conditionings that are preventing you from becoming a god or goddess.

Since God is the only Being in existence that has the ability to create or cause change to occur, and we were made in God's image. We will have the ability to do the same thing God has done on a smaller scale, but only if we mimic our Creator in exactness. This is the whole purpose of life and it is the reason you are here.

Spirituality 101

Just to recap what was said in the previous chapters. Everything that exists came from the essence, power or Spirit of God who is the creator of all things. The Divine is the creator of the physical and spiritual realm, which makes up our universe. We are a direct reflection of our universe. Hence we are a microcosm of a greater Macrocosm. The pure essence of God resides in the spiritual realm at the Amun Ra moment of the maa aankh, which means it lies deep beyond our physical conception and deep within our being. The pure essence of God is indestructible and it manifests itself within our being as our soul called the ab. The spiritual realm of the universe manifests itself as our unconscious, superconscious, higher self, or higher spirit, the divine spark within called the ba. The physical realm of the universe manifests itself as our subconscious, lower self, lower spirit, the brain, the physical body awareness, the false self, or the ego called our sahu.

Spiritual enlightenment is just a fancy way of saying connecting back to the Divine. It is being used throughout this text out of convenience, because we are never truly disconnected from the Divine. This is because God is everywhere and in everything, since God created everything. It is only when we shift our ab awareness to our sahu that we fall for the illusion that we are disconnected from God and from all of the other living beings on the planet. When we feel that we are disconnected from God and from all of the living things. We focus totally on our selfish needs and desires by surrounding ourselves with nothing but things. These things then become what we identify with and they define who we are. When our ab is shifted to our sahu, we tend to believe that the things we have, make us who we are. The dilemma of course that we get in is that when we lose these things such as our job, money, cars and begin to have problems with our health.

73

We fall under the belief that we are powerless and cannot succeed without these things. This of course is not true, but we only believe this when we allow our sahu to lead our life.

We therefore have to learn how to live from our ba and not our sahu. If we live from the sahu, we will always feel that we have to compete for everything because we don't see our connection to the Divine and all living beings. When you choose to live from your ba you will realize that you don't have to fight for what you want, because God has already provided it for you. It is just a matter of making a way for it to physically manifest. This means what you want and need is already yours. It already exists spiritually, because it was conceived in your mind. As soon as you imagined it (or saw it with your third eye) it was conceived. Now, we just have to make it a physical reality. It is just a matter of putting yourself in the right state of mind to obtain it, hence living from the head and not the tail.

A lot of people misunderstand what spirituality is all about. They think that being spiritual means putting out into the atmosphere what you want or begging God to give you what you want, while they just sit back, meditate and wait for what they want to come. Sorry, it doesn't work that way. True spirituality means listening and following the Spirit. It consists of you being a steward of God or God's servant. Now this doesn't mean that you are just a mindless drone just doing whatever intuitively comes to you, like a divine puppet. No, to be a vessel of God means you understand that you are connected to the Divine, so to help yourself you have to help others. The question that comes to mind is how do you shift to the ba and become a vessel of God? Well, the answer is that we can take one of three paths.

The Three Paths to POWER

It should be clear now that the reason we were created in the image of God is so that the Will of the Divine can be expressed through us. This is the reason we love to create, discover, draw, invent, paint, theorize, build, construct, write, and so on, because we are all expressing the divine spark within our being, but it takes us some time to come to this realization. Some of us come into this realization much sooner than

74

others, but eventually we will come into it because I believe there are three paths to reconnecting back to the Divine or three paths to Rau (POWER). Each of these paths, which I have modeled after my own personal experience, corresponds perfectly to the three crowns of Kamit.

Path of the Deshret Crown:
POWER by Struggle & Spirituality

The color red symbolizes fire, caution, hot, stop, aggression, activity and movement. On the color spectrum, the color red has the lowest frequency and therefore, the highest amount of negativity. It symbolizes the physical realm that we are all born into and the first road we all must take in reconnecting back to the God's Rau. Through this road, most of us discover how to connect to the Divine through some unfortunate circumstances. It is equivalent to the Jonah and the Fish story, but it is more like going through hell. For instance, before Malcolm X found the Divine, he experienced loss, separation, substance abuse, imprisonment and betrayal. There are other heroic individuals that experienced a great adversity that brought them into the divine fold.

I for instance, first came into my knowing after undergoing a major spiritual crisis. In fact, it was a spiritual dilemma that made me become interested in spiritual matters. For some people it could be the loss of a job that causes them to reconnect back to God. For others it could be imprisonment, a natural disaster like a tornado, the death of a loved one, etc. Whatever the case, when an individual gets on this path, it is usually not by choice, but due to some sort of problem, difficulty, setback, etc. That causes you to see the impurities of your soul.

As I mentioned in my own story, when I first learned about the maa aankh. It was after I became deathly ill. My ill-ness was a very humbling experience because I had to learn to listen to the Voice of God speaking within and depend upon others. If I had not had experienced this setback I would not have learned how to have faith in God and be conscientious of my words. Although I am not perfect (I have a lot to learn still), I am very optimistic and I am not selfish. I try

75

not to be arrogant or egotistical, and. I am more patient than I was several years ago.

So, the Deshret crown refers to coming into the Divine fold after undergoing some major ordeal. Most individuals called to be shamans undergo a similar ordeal where they become deathly ill or have to conquer some negative trait about them self in order to live. Whenever you are in dire straits, where everything seems to be going wrong or nothing seems to be going right. You are on the path of the Red Crown.

I remember prior to me becoming ill, things just seemed to not be going right. I mean there were all sorts of obstacles that were arising. Nothing was working. I was having problems with my coworkers, my supervisor didn't appreciate me and kept trying to get me do other jobs outside of my pay grade. When I was told to do something, I just bit my tongue and didn't say anything. Then went about my way and did what I was told out of resentment and fear that I might lose my job. The whole situation was making me become increasingly agitated and frustrated, which forced me to look for a way out, another job.

When I took the other job. I got paid less than what I was making at my previous one. It was the easy way out and I was relieved to not have to deal with my coworkers and supervisors, but shortly after. This new job had its host of problems, which contributed to my failing health, such as exposure to chemicals and a racially bias work environment. I realized after a couple of months of working there I should have stayed at my old job. I wanted to go back but I didn't want to seem as if I was begging for my old job. Shortly after that is when I became ill.

I know now that every time there is some form of direct or indirect suffering that occurs, rather it is an illness, natural disaster, layoffs, death, etc. It is a sign that you are on the Deshret path. The events that occur on this path are meant to get you to evaluate who you are and your connection to the Divine. If you connect or reconnect to the Divine and the link is strong. You will overcome the dilemma at hand because there is a change in consciousness. If your connection to the Divine is weak, these problems will seem to never go away and you will look for an easy way out, which will only make matters worse.

The Deshret path is the first path we encounter because it addresses our fears. When you are on this path, an easy way out will always present itself. I should have for instance, stood up and talked to my old supervisor about the work conditions, instead of searching for another job. When I gave into my fear, I gave into my sahu and was brought to a new low. The reason I didn't stand up and face my fear, which this path indicates is because I didn't have inner strength. Inner strength or courage is symbolized by the white Hedjet crown and comes from the ba. The key word of the Hedjet crown, which is djet, means "backbone" and "column" a pun on inner strength. It is the column displayed on the Osar truth sign in the previous exercise. This is why we all fail in some fashion or form to address issues correctly and instead take the easy way out. We simply need the djet.

It is important that you don't fool yourself into believing that God created this dilemma in order for you to reconnect back to the Rau. No, you through your ego created the situation for you to reconnect back to God. God just approved of it and respected your will. God has been speaking to you through your ba since you were a child. The reason you stop listening is because somewhere in our early lifetime we decided that we did not want listen and do our own thing. This road is a reminder of the choices we made so many years ago to live on our own distant from God. This is why the path of the Red Deshret Crown is technically the spiritual path where one faces obstacles and must learn to overcome trouble in order to find Self.

Path of the Hedjet Crown:
POWER by Consequence & Mysticism

As I mentioned in the previous paragraph, I was a changed man after my deathly ill-ness and near-death experience. I went to the hospital twice and on both occasions, my temperature was near critical, my breathing shallow and heartbeat faint. I was determined that I was not going a third time because three strikes and you're out. I determined or willed that I was not going to be rushed back to IC Unit, and that is how I came into the understanding that I had a say so if I was going to live or die. When I decided that I wanted to live. I could hear the Voice within me ask what I was willing to do in order to make it happen. So, I knew from that moment on that God supports us in whatever it is we want to do.

Forever changed by my previous experience made me realize that when something unexpected occurred to me. I simply had to readjust something in my life. I soon began to see that there are no such things as accidents and coincidences. Everything happens for a reason, regardless if we can see the purpose of it or not. I stopped watching certain programs that broadcasted imagery that did not remind of what I wanted or my divinity. And, I contemplated day and night. In fact every night, I spoke and listened to the Voice of God speaking within. This was almost complete 360-degree change from the way I was prior to becoming ill. I was a changed individual because I was goal driven. I wanted to be healed from my illness, so I did everything that was in my power to heal my body. This path made me very goal oriented.

When you are on this road you learn to develop patience. You learn how to contemplate (meditate), study, and so on because you are in a learning phase where you are listening to the Spirit. In this path an individual accepts that certain unexplainable events will occur. They are for the most part at peace with this because they have accepted that some of the events can be prevented, while those that cannot are simply outside of his or her control. This path is represented by the white Hedjet crown because an individual on this path knows they are connected to the Divine and looks forward to making miracles in the life. Actually, the individual on this path is not really making miracles. They are actually reproducing science, which is the reason why they are so astute when it comes to explaining and understanding metaphysical principles. They are looking for ways to reproduce similar results. For instance, an individual that is on this path understands after studying the cause and effects of things that "whatsoever they sow, they will reap." Now, they may not know why this principle works, but they know it works. It therefore, becomes a way to justify certain acts and behaviors.

To get an idea of how this individual lives when in a dire situation. They could lose everything but they have faith that they will get it back because they know nothing lasts forever and everything occurs in cycles. Their faith is the understanding of God and spiritual or metaphysical sciences, which develops in him or her inner strength.

Again, reflecting back on my experience, it took a little time for me to recover, but when I did. Talk about feeling great and powerful! I was on top of the world. Almost instantly, I got a better job that I enjoyed, which paid me more than I had expected. I got several promotions afterwards, which led to a full-time salary position. That's remarkable considering several years ago I was working a, regular eight-hour dead-end shifts, with mandatory occasional midnight shifts.

But, like I said, this path is all about goals. Now, there's nothing wrong with setting goals except it has a tendency to be used by the Enemy to disconnect us from the Divine. How you might be wondering? Well, what happens when the goals you set aren't met or don't come into fruition? What happens when you come in contact with someone that is not part of your plan and doesn't support your goals? If you are not careful, it is easy to fall and curse the Divine for not making something happen when you wanted it to. So, we have to move beyond this path and to the third path.

Path of the Pschent Crown: POWER by Resolve & Miracles

This road is called the white and red Pschent crown path because it centers on being in the world but not of the world or walking on the edge of both worlds – the physical and spiritual. It is a true heroic path because it involves living for a purpose. When you discover that you have a purpose in life. You will see that everything else has a purpose too. For instance, everything I went through from my illness and so on was meant to bring me to this point, so that I can share what little wisdom I have to help others. It took me a while to accept that I have the natural ability to teach and assist others, but when I finally settled into it. I began noticing that opportunities pertaining to my talents became readily available. This made me stop worrying about the future and convinced me that all I need to concern myself with is the present, so that I can take advantage of the opportunities I have.

I must inform you that one of the big differences between this road and the previous one, is that the latter is approached from a studious, trial and error perspective. It is like walking across a hidden land bridge with a staff, poking to see where solid ground stands. The Pschent road is like just having faith that there is solid ground wherever you walk. I must admit, it is a somewhat frightening path because faith is not an attribute well developed in many of us. I just recently embarked upon this road and have been compelled to help others even against my better judgment. The reason I didn't want to help them was because I didn't think that they would be interested in what I knew. My Osar on the other hand saw things differently, so I had to suck it up and share. The few times I did this, I did see miracles occur as people were transformed with this spiritual science. Most of the time I didn't and this is what my Osar was trying to reveal to me, that I have to stop depending upon and looking for instant gratification. Like a good educator, I had to trust that the skills I am teaching and sharing are improving the lives of others, because there is no instant gratification. I have to just have faith.

I learned that as I embarked upon this road that true blessings come from the Divine. The greatest reward comes from serving others, which helps in improving and benefiting you. Here lies the purpose of life, which is simply to be happy and at peace by reconnecting to the Divine. This road to enlightenment is a living path, where you truly walk by faith by following your spirit – your ba or Osar to improve your life and the lives of others.

We Are All Called

In essence what this means is that we are all *called* to fulfill a higher purpose because it is our duty, purpose, dharma or what the Kamitians called maa. The thing is, that we all have different callings. All of us are not called to do the same profession, but we are all called to help improve the lives of others. We are all called to be problem solvers and to enrich the lives of others with our unique purpose, our maa, because we are all children of the Most High. We just need to decide which path we want to take to answer the Call.

Most of the time when people hear or read something about a Calling they automatically equate it to something religious and spiritual, like being called to be a preacher or a shaman, because our contemporary Western society divides our reality into spiritual and secular categories. But, in actuality, the Calling can refer to any profession and anything that is long termed. For instance, you may be called to be a teacher. You may not be called to be a musician but instead a songwriter or music producer. You just never know unless you overcome your fear and reach out on faith.

Before we proceed, it must be understood that the Calling has nothing to do with your dreams. The Calling always has something to do with you overcoming a problem or some destructive experience, which occurred because of a change in consciousness and awareness. It can be a traumatic event that took place in your childhood or something as simple as seeing an individual victimize and deciding to take a stance against it.

The way it happens is that one-day you are going about your business say for instance, walking down the street where you routinely pass a park. At the park you see some guys on the playground that you think are peddling drugs. You think nothing about it, so you go about your business. The next day, you walk down the street, pass the park and see the same guys on the playground peddling drugs. Again, you don't think about it, so you continue on your way. Day after day, you go through the same routine and the more you pass by the park and see the playground, the more you wonder about the guys at the playground. Then something clicks. One day while walking down the street and passing the playground you begin to wonder why aren't any children playing there and you notice how dangerous the environment has become. Something inside you begins to spark and begins to make you imagine how this playground could be a better place. This is how the Calling begins and at this moment you can do one or two things. You can either ignore the Call or you can follow the spark within and try to make the playground a better place.

So you see the Calling doesn't just refer to some epic change in whom we are. It can be anything that strikes a chord with us and compels us to take the initiative to make life better for all. A prime example of how a following the Calling can take a little event and turn it into a worldwide phenomenon can be seen in the Rosa Parks story. Whether or not she was the first minority in the Jim Crow south, to refuse to give up her seat to a white patron is not important. The significant point about her story in regards to the Calling is that she got tired of seeing an injustice being committed and decided to do something about it.

Now, here is a scary thought. Imagine what would have happen if Rosa Parks never answered her Calling. Imagine how different the world would be if she had chosen to stand or go to the back of bus as usual.

Who Is Calling You?

We have all heard people talk about how an individual is called but who is the one doing the Calling? Before answering this question first let's discuss a few things that have been occurring to help us understand this phenomenon.

In recent years, there have been a lot of reports from all around the world, about peoples' guardian angels appearing to them in a time of need. Many of these stories are astonishing, as people had indicated how their life was spared due to their angel intervening on their behalf. The interesting thing is that when these people tell their tales of how they avoided an accident, were awaken in the middle of the night and escaped a fire or even led down a corridor on 9/11 before the towers crashed. They don't all describe their angels as being some winged figure with a halo hovering in the ether. Many have indicated that their guardian angel was a deceased loved one like a loving grandparent, aunt, uncle or someone they were close to in life. Others describe these guardian angels as bright and blinding orbs of light.

But it makes one wonder, why do these angels appear only in dire circumstances. Why when we are in danger do these mysterious beings appear out of nowhere to give us guidance and direction? Is it possible that these ethereal beings could further assist us and take a more prominent role? Well, I found the answer to this question in the *Story of Osar*.

If you will recall that when Set first usurped the throne no one directly opposed him as he spread terror throughout the land. This part of the story is an allusion of how we give into our lower spirit – our sahu – whenever we refuse to take responsibility for our actions and what's wrong in the world. Whenever we tend to look the other way or take a blind eye and ignore what is going on. We are just as guilty as those who support Set in his actions. When we finally decide to oppose the enemy this is when we receive divine assistance in fighting Set.

The *Story of Osar* indicates that every action we take has its consequences. This is very important to understand because when we deny that evil exists in our homes, communities, organizations, etc. We invite evil to take a more active role in our life, which hinders our spiritual transformation. Our refusal to fight evil on whatever level encourages the Confederates of Set to take up camp in our lives. These conspirators are what most people refer to as the bad angels, which the Kamitic thinkers called *aapepu*, metaphorically described as being venomous snakes and worms. When however we choose to stand up against Set – our deeds, feelings and thoughts have a positive consequence, which encourages the good angels to come into our life. These good angels are what the Kamitic thinkers called *aakhu*[18] (our ancestral spirits and spirit guides) and *netcharu* (guardian angels).

Now when some people first hear this, the first thing they ask in disbelief is, "How is all of the suffering in the world their fault or the result of an individual's thoughts?" The short and sweet answer is that our thoughts generate our actions, which is why it is so important that

---

[18] Aakhu is the general term used for referring to benevolent and revered ancestors, while aapepu is the term used to refer to ancestral spirits that committed major crimes against humanity such as adultery murder and theft.

83

we raise our consciousness. When we do not and we refuse to accept responsibility for the ill, it will contribute the problem. But, still this answer does not explain how and why evil exists to most people. The reason is because our sahu was programmed to help us to survive by learning and mimicking others. In its attempt to learn from others, it also tries to solve problems but this is not its purpose, which is why there are thousands of theories that exists about one subject. We have to learn that in order to resolve some problems we need to hand it over to the wisest part of our being – our ba. The only way to do this is by focusing on the solution and not the hows and whys. When you focus on the hows and whys, you give power to the problem and not the solution. I have never met anyone that avoided becoming ill by focusing on how and why they become ill. I have on the other hand, met a number of people have become healthy by focusing on improving and perfecting their health.

What this means is that the one calling us to do better is a combination of factors. From one perspective, we can say it is God, on the other hand since our benevolent actions and behaviors causes our good angels – our aakhu (ancestors) and netcharu (guardian angels) – to take a more active role in our life. It can be said that our angels our calling us, so that they can manifest themselves physically through us. I on the other hand, personally think that life calls us and the reason is because it is how we set it up. That's right, we called our self.

You see keeping in mind that what makes us divine is that we have an ab – soul, which gives us free will or the ability to make choices and decisions. So, prior to being born into this physical world, we made the decision along with God, our aakhu and netcharu to have specific obstacles set up by Set in our life in order to accomplish certain objectives. I imagine we all met in the spiritual realm and God stated that something needed to be done because it is part of the Divine Plan and the Divine asked, "I need a volunteer?"

So, we chose to be here and this became our destiny or maa, but in order to accomplish the goals that God had set. When we were born into the physical realm, all memory of our destiny had to be erased, in order to be fair to ourselves. If memory of our destiny were not erased, our life would be like playing a set of fixed games that we

84

know we are going to win. It would be boring because we wouldn't have any challenges or real opposition that we need to overcome in order to win the game. We would know everything that is going to happen before it happens. So we are born into this physical realm with a clean slate sort of speak. While those on the other side, such as our aakhu remember our destiny because they didn't have it erased from their memory. This is why we need God, the netcharu and our aakhu, but at the same time God, the netcharu and our aakhu need us to fulfill the task we promised to do.

Why Are We Being Called?

Now, the beseeching question that most of us want to know is why were we called in the first place? It is simple. It is to bring a bit of KAMTA or the Kingdom of Osar into the physical realm. KAMTA it must be remembered is a perfect and pure realm, which is where the Spirit of God resides. We have to remember that every time we do something that is right and just, we bring back a little of Osar's knowledge and wisdom to improve the lives of people in TASETT. This means that when we are ill and we recover from the illness. We have visited Osar and returned to help others with the same problem. When an individual has been imprisoned and has a true change in consciousness. They can return back to the land of the living to help others avoid the same mistakes that they made, which led them to their incarceration. We are called to erect new models from KAMTA that will help people in TASETT. We learn these models from visiting our aakhu who reside in the Kingdom of Osar in KAMTA.

You see, some of the models we have for living are like healthy trees producing good and healthy fruit. For instance, if you have a good model for how a family is supposed to conduct their family affairs. It is because your aakhu (ancestors) provided you with a good example on how to do this. Meaning your aakhu when they were alive when it came to family matters discussed issues reasonably. They didn't cuss and fight each other and swear not to speak to each other until death. They came together as a family and worked to help one another out. For this reason, one of your jobs as their descendant is to maintain the

85

model they left by teaching it to the younger generations, so that they will continue to bear good fruit in their life.

But, all of our aakhu weren't perfect. Some of our aakhu left behind some baggage and a whole lot of mess for the living to clean up, which we call nowadays "dysfunctional." It is a documented fact that most children that grow up in an abusive home become abusive adults themselves. Individuals that were emotionally abused, end up being "walked" on by others who are more dominant. People who grew up in an environment where alcohol and drugs abuse is commonplace, may not detest substance abuse but instead become addicted to other things like food and so on. All of these problems occur in an individual's life because they didn't have a proper model to show them otherwise. Simply put, if you never saw how to resolve problems by clearing your head. You would've concluded that the only way to resolve the problem is to suppress it with alcohol and drugs. The same applies for emotional, physical, and substance abuse. A lot of relationships have been damaged because of a combination of these issues along with the unhealthy paradigm promoted by fairytales, which imply that women are just supposed to sit on their throne and dictate what they want, while their husband works and provides them with everything they desire.

If you were provided a good model and by good, I mean a system that shows you how to resolve issues from a calm, peaceful and productive manner. Most likely you are either married or have someone in your life that doesn't have a working model them self. This is one of the individuals that you are supposed to help and in the same token they are supposed to help you as well because when we have a dysfunction in our lives it is usually due to a family curse. The way to deal with family curses is discussed in the exercise below, but the point being made is this is why you were called.

Who Are Our Ancestors?

A lot has been said about our aakhu (ancestors) but the real question is who and what are they? Well, the Kamitic philosophers described them as being the stars in night sky, meaning they are the little spiritual

86

energies that help guide us through life, but this is just the general understanding of what an ancestor is. When we look at the term aakhu it translates to "light, splendor, splendid acts, brilliance, virtues, excellences, glorious deeds, benefits, blessings, to become a spirit, endowed with spirit, a saintly spirit, glorified spirit," and so on. The term aakhu is as a prefix and suffix in a number of Kamitic words referencing the sun, Hru as well as animals that are known to be aggressive, strong willed and protective such as Aakhutenaten, aakhut heh, and the Kamitic netcharu of defense Hruaakhuti. What this implies is that in short, an aakhu is a brilliant and splendid warrior spirit of the dead.

Basically an ancestor is a warrior, but the reason most of us don't see our ancestors as warriors is because we think of warriors from a Western perspective as being an individual that physically fights against others. But a warrior is anyone that is troubled in life and fights to persevere to the end. In other words, an aakhu is our role model, but these role models are not like the athletes, singers and other entertainers that we pick today as models of how we should do things. They are the individuals that shape our culture and the spiritual progress of the people by raising the consciousness of others. They are typically individuals that we think about in our times of uncertainty because of their inner strength. The ancestors exist as clans in the heavenly realm of KAMTA.

To understand this it is said in the Yoruba tradition of West Africa that we all come from a "heavenly grouping." This same belief is expressed in Christianity, which teaches that God has many mansions. This means that when people are born on the planet. They all have similar beliefs, backgrounds, experiences and aspirations, because they are coming from the same or similar heavenly house. This is why it shouldn't be a coincidence that when an event occurs. There are a number of people supporting it. For instance the outlawing of slavery all occurred in around the early 1800s throughout most of the world. The abolishing of slavery throughout the West in general occurred around the mid to the late 1800s and so on as if there was a mass movement to change peoples' awareness.

87

Another example of this can be seen in how in African American culture from slavery, to the Harlem Renaissance, followed by the Civil Rights and Black Power Movements. There was a host of people supporting these different events, which laid the foundation for younger generations to follow.

So our aakhu are the individuals that created the cultural models of how we should act, behave; conduct our affairs and so on. Many of these cultural models can be found throughout the Afro-Diaspora but African American spirituality is quite distinct from their Caribbean and Latin American kin, because it developed in Protestant North America where most of the other cultural traditions developed in a predominantly Roman Catholic setting. As a result, African American spirituality is an interesting mixed of Traditional African beliefs and practices, combined primarily with Pentecostal and Holiness influences, which were borrowed from the brief Spiritualism stint that passed through the United States; Peppered with other religious beliefs like Catholicism and the self-empowerment through self-sufficiency teachings of Elijah Muhammad. To understand how this interesting mixture came about we have to look at how African American spirituality developed in North America.

In some traditions, while it is claimed that your aakhu (ancestors) are only supposed to include your blood relatives, when the Africans were brought to the Americas. A new definition of family was created in order for early African Americans to survive. This is because prior to being brought to the Americas, the Africans were very communal and respect was paid to one's parents, grandparents, the leader of one's clan and other hierarchy in the African society. When the Africans arrived in North America. Many of them tried to maintain this social structure with their family and tribal ties, as other Africans had done in Cuba and Brazil, but to prevent possible uprisings and encourage disparity. Slave owners systematically destroyed early African American social structures and family institutions by selling family members to other slave owners in another part of the country (sometimes in another country). To get an idea how this happened, any slave that was respected too much by other slaves was viewed as a potential threat and was simply sold to another slave owner. It is believed by some historians that the slave-owner also deliberately

88

created differences amongst their slaves by raping the women and sodomizing some of the men in the slave community. As a result, children of mixed ethnicity were viewed as being black because of the One-drop rule[19], but it was believed however that they would create cultural difference amongst the slaves.

To protect against this cultural attack, early African Americans realized that they couldn't follow the same cultural model as they had done in their homeland, because they were in a foreign land, living as captives in tyranny, with no tribal leaders, no priesthood, and no kingship. Since, everyone that had some significant role in Africa was now a slave and the strongest were constantly being sold to other plantation owners so that they didn't incite any insurrection. A new cultural model needed to be created to survive slavery. Due to the fact that the elders of the slave community were more knowledgeable about the old ways and considered the most trusted by the slave owners. The new leaders became these individuals commonly known as Uncle "So-and-so" and Aunt or Big Momma. They were the patriarch and matriarchs of the slave community. It was because of these individuals that when a void was created by the slave master's whim, to sell a member of the family, a relative or some other responsible individual in the community filled it. This is how other cultures and individuals outside of one's family lineage was adopted into the new African American concept of family. An ancestor or aakhu from the early African American perspective shortly after became an individual that significantly influenced your life for the better. Although most aakhu are our biological ancestors the following is a list of other aakhu circulating around your space:

- Cultural aakhu are the ancestral spirits that established the cultural model that many of our families follow today. They are the Uncles, Aunts, Big Dad and Big Mommas that maintained our family culture. In an attempt to make Christian whites sympathetic to the slave's plight, Harriet Beecher Stowe wrote

---

[19] The One-drop rule was the social classification used in North America that meant if an individual had any African ancestry they were considered black. The rule was not officially adopted as a law until the early 20th century.

Uncle Tom's Cabin, which was very influential in convincing people that slavery was not Christian-like. But, it also created a stereotypical myth about African American way of life, which led to the creation of racist stereotypical imagery. The truth is that the real Uncle and Mammies were respected members in the community.

❖ The real Uncle in the black community was a field hand that was never allowed near the slaveholders' house because of his magical knowledge. They were called Uncle because it was their responsibility to pass along oral tradition to younger generation and prepare them for the hostile environment they would soon be entering. The real Uncles had white hair symbolizing their wisdom. They corresponded to the Luvemba moment, the setting sun of the Kongo Cross (or Ra Atum on the Maa Aankh). They are the epitome of the Kongo ancestor N'Zambi and the Kamitic ancestor Osar. For more information see the Uncle Remus stories.

❖ The real Aunties and Big Mommas who worked as cooks, maidservants, etc. were master herbalists (since healthcare for slaves rarely existed), midwives, skilled fortunetellers and seers. Using the psychic abilities they provided guidance for the people. This strong psychic trait is one of the reasons women were highly regarded in traditional African society. The tradition originated in Kamit with Oset (Auset, Isis).

• Teaching aakhu, which are aakhu that you acquire and help you to learn various disciplines and skills, such as the deceased master of a martial arts system. This could be a teacher that first interested you in mathematics or a famous dancer. To honor these spirits you might offer them some a candle and ask them to help you in their chosen field of study. A teaching aakhu doesn't necessarily have to be a professional. It could be a neighbor, the friend of the family, etc. that taught you how to play basketball, etc. I have found in my experience that teaching spirits a lot of times come from other traditions especially after we have encountered another culture. This spirit could be the Chinese Kuan Yin who comes to teach you about being compassionate and merciful. If you encountered Hawaiian traditions, visited or happened to be visiting Hawaii, Pele, who is known throughout the islands to visit indigenous and visitors alike, to warn you about future danger. If you encounter a number of Hispanics and Latinos who are Catholics, a Catholic saint could visit and teach you. Like the spirit San Alejo was taught me about perseverance. Many times they will sit your aakhu unless you get instruction for them to be elevated.

A final word about teaching aakhu is that when one appears, you have every right to question who that aakhu is especially since it is not part of your immediate bloodline. Most aakhu understand your skepticism and will not object. Ask the aakhu who they are, where they are from and ask them something that you don't know that can be verified like a historical, philosophical or cultural fact. If the teaching aakhu appears and is braggart, claiming to once be very powerful, most likely it is not an aakhu but an aapepu in disguise. Often times they will reveal themselves to you in the way you are use to receiving spiritual information such as in a dream.

- Native American aakhu are the spirits of Amerindians, the original inhabitants of the Americas. During slavery some Native Americans had African slaves because they saw that this institution was not going to go away any time soon. These slaves however were allowed to enter into the Native American society and adopt various Indian customs. There were other Native Americans during slavery that hid African runaways from enslavers and allowed them to enter into their society, as well. This brave act is honored by the Mardi Gras Indians of New Orleans. As a result, Native American aakhu have a tendency to visit the altar where it is still believe they serve as lookouts, concealers and scouts. Many of the Native American aakhu when their icons are placed upon the altar or some other space, will sit quiet in contemplation and rarely speak, meaning you will rarely get an impression from them. When you get an idea from them it is pretty profound, then they go back to being silent, cautious, watchful and observant. When you receive insight from them, you should thank them by giving them an offering. They are fond of cigar or pipe tobacco smoke, which means you shouldn't abuse this herb since it is sacred to them. They are also fond of sage. Most Native Americans spirits of North American origin do not accept alcoholic beverages but prefer water. Many of them walk with the netchar Maat but they can be found surrounding any of the netchar. You just have to trust your intuition.

Another interesting thing about Native American aakhu that I have recently discovered is that because Native Americans have always protested the illegal occupation of their land, the mass killing of the beast and fowl, and the injustice done on their people, as seen by the most famous of Native American aakhu Black Hawk. They continue to revolt, but also hide runaways in KAMTA known collectively as the "unknown and forgotten." How this came about I am not sure. What comes to mind is that when they found runaway slaves who died and they still gave the individual a proper burial. Consequently, those who died violently but saw the error in their ways are still sheltered by these spirits it seems. These "unknown and forgotten" spirits can be very rude and wild. You can sense their presence whenever you begin to have strange dreams, visions and thoughts. Spraying ammonia around sacred space with a spritzer bottle can rid your surrounding of the very unruly. Also, a rue plant or spray made of rue tea may also be helpful.

The great thing about Native American aakhu is that because mainstream America has finally begun to take responsibility for the wrong committed against Native Americans. Their cultural influence is semi-appreciated so you it is not strange to find Native American artwork all over the place. This means that a Native American statue can be put in the public view, without them knowing that this aakhu is a scout watching over you.

- Historical aakhu (ancestors that have made history and are an inspiration to generations). We are familiar with these aakhu because we usually hear and read about them in history class or some other event.

- Mythical aakhu are ancestral spirits inspired by religious traditions. The line between these spirits and the netcharu blurs at times because the factual story of their origin has been lost and all that exist is myth. In the end, mythical aakhu end up becoming archetypes. From this perspective, the netcharu are actually mythical aakhu.

These are the aakhu that make themselves known in African American community. Please note that while these aakhu may resemble or appear very similar to the aakhu in other spiritual traditions. They are not exactly the same. For instance, unlike the Caribbean and Latin America were Asians and Arabs worked as indentured servants and shared their culture with others. North America was a segregated country and even though cultural influences were shared in some areas. The segregation of the country prevented a massive intermixing of cultures. This does not mean that you cannot pay homage to spirit from another culture. It simply means that you should be very skeptical to ensure that this spirit is legit and not an aapepu in disguise.

The Difference between the Calling & Our Dreams

Sometimes it is difficult to distinguish between our Calling and our dreams. The difference between the two is that the latter refers to personal goals and objectives that we set for our self. Most of the time, these goals and objectives are usually ego based such as to have a specific job, to have a certain type of house, drive a certain type of car, etc. Your Calling as I stated has more to do with your awareness and the awareness of others. For instance, when there is a problem occurring in a community, it is because most people aren't aware of the imbalance it is causing for everyone. Just think about how people began to realize that if they poisoned the lakes, rivers and oceans, we poison ourselves, which led to a massive environmental movement. So, the Calling refers to a change in awareness of usually yourself and others.

93

One way to distinguish between the Calling and your dreams is usually your Calling comes pretty natural. It is something that you have the skills and talents to do. This doesn't mean that it is going to be incredibly easy; it just means that you shouldn't feel overwhelmed. If you feel overwhelmed like you can't do it then you may not be on the correct path. When you answer your Calling you should feel like you are the right man or woman for the job, but that you have a lot of work to do.

Another way to recognize your Calling is that it is usually the thing you don't want to do, or can't imagine yourself doing. Even though you will find that you are a natural at doing it. As I have mentioned before, I never would have imagined myself being a teacher but it is one of the roles that I have found myself in and I learned that I am quite good at it. When I look back and try to explore why I didn't want to go into this profession. It was because how teachers were treated and the low rate of pay, which you can clearly see was an ego-driven response.

I know you are probably wondering that if our Calling deals with serving the needs of others then what about our dreams. Is it wrong to want a nice house, nice car and other nice things? The answer is no. It is not wrong to have material things. The thing is that we have to find a way to link our dreams with our Calling. In other words, we have to see how we can accomplish our dreams by helping others. This is where the challenge lies. One way to do this is by figuring out what you really want you by distinguishing between what you need and what you desire. According to psychologist Abraham Maslow's *Hierarchy of Needs'* we all have five basic needs that we are always trying to fulfill. They are listed from the greatest to the least important:

1. Self- actualization Needs: the need for self – fulfillment, creativity, morality and ability to solve problems
2. Esteem Needs: self – achievement, confidence, respect for and by others
3. Social Needs: acceptance, affection, intimacy and love
4. Safety Needs: protection from physical, natural, material, financial, economical, and emotional harm
5. Physiological Needs: food, water, shelter, sleep, air, sex, etc.

Most of our wants I believe register at the number one position because most of us do not know how to achieve our goal once it is set. So, in order to get what we want, we have to find what motivates us and what we are passionate about.

Contrary to popular belief, we are not all supposed to like everything. Some people enjoy reading and writing, others enjoy math, while some don't like either. You have to be honest with yourself and get real. If you don't like math there is no way you are going to be interested in anything that is math related like engineering, unless you develop a love for math. If you are a people person, then you need to go into a people person field. If you aren't a people person and find yourself at a job in sales, you can do all the spiritual work you want, but you are going to fail because your heart is not in it. Get into something that you like. When you get into a field that you enjoy, you don't mind learning more about it in order to succeed because you are in your zone.

As I wrote in *Maa Aankh* volume one, I had all sorts of jobs and I wanted to be successful in them all, but no matter what I did I kept failing. It wasn't until I started teaching that I realized that the reason I had great luck dealing with people and writing, was because I was a natural teacher. When I really learned something I could really teach others and find all sorts of ways to get them to understand the subject. I was a natural when it came to teaching because I knew how to strike a chord within a person. When I accepted this I got promotion after promotion in the education field, and I am still receiving accolades. But this doesn't mean much to me because I am doing what I enjoy.

We all have a knack for something because it coincides with our purpose of being here. Don't try to force yourself to do something that you do not have a natural knack for. A lot of kids that leave home for college do this thinking they want to be a doctor, because doctors make a lot of money; knowing good and well that they don't like science. Don't do this and encourage others not to do this either. Most kids that grow up to be doctors started showing their aptitude when they were kids, not when they went to college. So, don't do this to yourself. Before doing anything, you need to first find what your knack is. The sooner you find your knack, the less time you will spend and money you will waste pursuing goals that weren't meant for you. This will also help you get the things that you want, but also help you to identify what you were called to do.

Acknowledging the Calling

The great thing about the Calling is that you don't have to go find it. It is you because it is your purpose for being here. Everything that you do relates to your Calling, even if you think it doesn't. For instance, if you see the dangers of street gangs and you find that your purpose is to help young people avoid the trappings of getting into street gangs. Then that becomes your purpose because you see the pitfalls it leads to. It then becomes your responsibility to help as many people as possible to avoid this destructive way of life. It is your dharma, your maa.

If you fail to acknowledge your maa, then matters will only become worse until you do because the Calling has a lot to do with your awareness. This is the reason the maa on the maa aankh cosmogram as a bridge between the Amun Ra and Ra moments. It indicates that once you have that epiphany, that aha moment, the flash of insight represented as the Amun Ra moment. You have to immediately act upon it, signified by the Ra moment or it will lead to Ra Atum, which is the downfall where serious change must be take place.

The traditional way to acknowledge the Calling is to build an altar, but the true purpose of building the altar is never explained, so let me shed some light on this. Usually when someone is called, Set, with his weapons of doubt, fear, etc. visits us in an attempt to discourage us from creating positive change. This is why every time an individual is called they go through a period of denial. So, the purpose of building the altar is to first acknowledge that you got the Call and second to hold the enemies of Osar at bay[20]. The building of an altar is also a

---

[20] The astute reader will recall that the first thing that Oset and Nebhet did after collecting the body parts of Osar was to erect a shrine, where the bodily remains were collected.

humbling experience because it symbolizes that you recognize you cannot physically create the change by yourself. You need some divine assistance, some real POWER, so it is a plea to the invisible, spiritual realm of KAMTA. Last but not least, the altar creates a doorway for your aakhu (benevolent ancestors) and netcharu (guardian spirits) to assist you in answer the Call. The whole altar building experience is based upon the *Story of Osar* when Oset and Nebhet, led by Npu (Anubis) found a piece of Osar's body and erected a shrine.

You have to understand that when you hear the Calling you are being given a chance and an opportunity to become an instrument of change. Now I know what some of you are thinking. You are wondering is it absolutely necessary for you to build an altar in order to answer your Calling and the answer is no it is not. The purpose of building the altar is that it makes obtaining your goals easier because if you will recall. Our sahu (the lower spirit and subconscious part of our being) has to be repetitively shown what we want it to do. The altar is the traditional way to build up our confidence and resolve.

Exercise 5:
How to Accept the Call

Before you accept the call it must be kept firmly in mind that what you are doing is acknowledging that most of your problems in your life are due to erroneous beliefs, ideas, models, etc. that you have learned and are stored in your sahu. In order to change or correct the beliefs, ideas, behaviors and models, you need to replace the old, outdated, useless and destructive beliefs, ideas, behaviors and models with new ones. To begin, to show your aakhu (ancestors and spirit guides) that you have accepted the call, you need to build a spiritual altar, which is called in this practice a Het Aakhu (Ancestral Spiritual House).

An altar is basically a consecrated and marked space where a human being enters into dialogue with the Divine and anything that is spiritual. It is one of the human characteristics that distinguish us from animals. Altars come in different sizes, shapes and forms. They can be places of nature or manmade. Traditionally speaking natural altars are where people go to resolve problems associated with their development. For instance, because mountains bring people closer to the sky, they were ideal for communicating with the Divine about spiritual growth and ethical behavior. Rivers and streams were places people would visit for all types of fertility issues since fresh water was used to grow crops and natural birth was facilitate in water. The forest and wilderness is where hunters usually went to provide food and would develop new tools to either hunt or be used as a weapon. Places that had been struck by lightning or had a natural fire presence were typically seen as places of transformation. But, when people began to migrate and were not able to visit these places of nature. They began creating altar spaces to symbolize and remind them of the essence that can only be found in nature.

In Kamta human made altars have two purposes. The first is to be a middle ground where KAMTA and TASETT meet, thereby bridging these two realities together. When you stand before your altar you are basically walking on the road of Maa (faith) and standing on the edge of two lands. The second purpose of the altars is to remind you who you are, which is, a divine being made in the image of God and a microcosm of a greater Macrocosm. This is the foundation behind working with the spirits because you have to see yourself as a god or goddess or a spirit amongst other spirits. More will be said about this in the latter part of the book.

The altar in Kamta is called a *het* (Kamitic for house) and it is imagined as being a spiritual house or mansion where one's ancestors have ascended to, referring to the biblical scripture that, "In my Father's House are many mansions[21]." The het is imagined as being a two-story, multilevel house or a tribal community in KAMTA with the bottom floor presided over by our aakhu and the second by our netcharu. Everyone has spiritual lineage or a spiritual clan that they descend from. We therefore, are the last living links of our ancestral line. When we have children they become the last living links and this is symbolized by the het, which pays homage to our ancestors and spiritual clan heads, the netcharu.

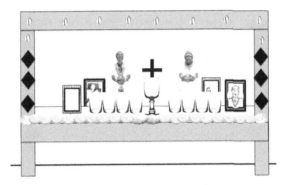

Figure 14: Spiritual House for the Aakhu & Netcharu

---

[21] The physical world significance of this is that no one should be able to enter and setup shop in community. If they can you do not have a community but a neighborhood and run the risk of being taken advantage of. The same therefore applies spiritually.

I will explain the symbolism behind this altar shortly. First you will begin by building the bottom tier or floor of your het. To construct it what you need is:

- A large clear goblet and eight glasses of water to symbolize the nine netcharu, the nine directions and nine major spiritual forces that exist in the universe. Kamta provides that each individual is connected with the nine netcharu that will accompany each individual through his or her life. Different aakhu associated with the netcharu will come in and out of our lives depending upon what we are doing, the task at hand or path that we are on. The water is used to clarify the channels for spiritual communication to easily take place and provide spiritual nourishment. The water in the glasses should be kept full throughout the week (if at all possible) and replaced at least once a week. The largest goblet is always placed in the middle, with the four glasses placed to the left (symbolizing the masculine aspect of nature) and four to the right (symbolizing the feminine aspect of nature). The water helps to keep the aakhu cool, relaxed and peaceful. When it is time to refresh the water. I have found that you can pour the old water from the glasses into the soil of your protective plants, since these plants have the ability to diffuse negative energies and spirits. For more information on your protective plants see the section on the Evil Eye.

- A small table, box, bookshelf or any flat surface that has been cleaned of debris. The surface of the altar can be covered with a white tablecloth, if you prefer. I favor painting the surface white over a tablecloth because when incense ashes or anything else falls on the altar. It makes it easier to clean up versus having to dismantle the altar just to wash the tablecloth. (Please note that the above design on the altar is used for decorative purposes only. Diamonds shapes were often used by African Americans to symbolize the safe evolution of their soul. The diamond like the cross in early African American thinking symbolized protection).

- An Eye of Djahuti (Aabit – the Eye of the Moon as a symbol of trance reminding one to go within), the Eye of Ra (Aakhu – the Eye of the Sun to remind one that this is where their true power derives

100

from), an ankh, a bare crucifix or even a star to represent Amun Ra.

- Male ancestors are placed on your left and female ancestors are placed on the right. It is also customary to put a figurine of an old African man and woman to symbolize the first ancestors brought to the Americas, whose wisdom survives even in this tradition[22]. These are the patriarch and matriarch of your family lineage. The ones responsible for the survival of your culture. They are your Uncle and Auntie or Big Dad and Big Momma.

- White seashells[23] are used to form a border (symbolizing the spiritual realm). The analogy is that the shells are used to protect the sacred within, as well as what is on the outside out. Shells are also a reminder that we come from the cosmic ocean of nyun (kalunga) and therefore, symbolize the horizontal line on the Maa Ankh. For extra potency the seashells can be covered with cascarilla, efun or white pemba (consecrated chalks that can be purchased at most Latin American spiritual supply stores) or regular chalk if none is available.

- A glass ashtray should be filled with sand to hold incense and cigars.

- White candles the size of birthday candles and cigars.

- A small jar or cup to be filled with Florida Water and other personal colognes or perfumes.

- A white coffee cup and saucer for food offerings. You may find yourself giving your aakhu strong black coffee or tea. Different traditions claim that the coffee or tea should or shouldn't be hot. I

---

[22] Kamitic spirituality is always about balance. Maa is always in the picture balancing energies and forces.
[23] In most Afro-Latino traditions chalk was used to mark off sacred space, but African Americans lacking the available African resources used instead naturally white or painted white seashells. The color white is the color of the white Hedjet crown symbol of knowledge, wisdom, purity and strength.

personally don't like cold coffee and I know that none of my aakhu who drank the stuff while they were alive liked cold coffee either, but there are some devotees that feel otherwise. Most traditions do agree that whichever beverage is given. It should be offered straight with no milk, cream or sugar and when the dishes aren't being used. They should be kept separate from your regular dishes.

- A bible (New Living Translation Bible if you are new to reading it) or Book of Psalms and Proverbs. Remember our intention is for spiritual practice and since most of our spirits were Christian or familiar with this faith. Our aakhu referred to the bible as the great "Conjuring Book' because they understood how to read it. They didn't take all that was written within literally, like the *Pert em Hru* (the so-called Egyptian Book of the Dead). They used it to create change. Many of us have bitter feelings because of how our oppressors have used the bible, but we need to get over it. Sorry there is no other way of saying. It is what our aakhu were familiar with. You need to ask them to help you to get over this if you are having problems accepting it. Now, if you choose not to, you can by all means use the *Pert em Hru* or some other inspirational religious texts. You should note however that by doing so since your immediate aakhu didn't speak the Kamitic language. You will have to teach them about it as you are learning about it yourself. It is a great learning experience and teaching your aakhu is really powerful and uplifting. I remember, I had to explain to my aakhu what I was missing and hope to obtain, before I could get the assistance of many of my Christian aakhu. It was a challenge. It was only after proving to them that the Kamitic tradition was the inspiration behind the Christian religion and show how the two were similar, that "some" of my aakhu conceded (not all). This is why trying to teach them about a foreign text may be even more challenging. If you are able to educate them it is a good thing and you will be able to sense progress.

I had an aakhu for instance who knew nothing about Npu – the Opener of the Way and Provider of Opportunity (which we will see in future chapters), but he wanted his photo placed near him there for the time being. After a month or so, this aakhu wanted to be placed on the ancestral altar. You see, we need to get out of the

102

habit of imposing our beliefs on our aakhu and accept that what they did, they did because that is what they had available to them at the time. When danger strikes and emergency is knocking on your front door, which one do your prefer? Would you prefer to rely upon theory and what you think might work, or what you know and have historical proof what worked? I prefer the latter.

- You will need some uplifting music like drumming, southern gospel, praise & worship, spirituals, folk, Latin (Cuban, Puerto Rican, Brazilian, etc.) Espiritisimo music, etc. Music is very important because just like today, regardless of beliefs, music is the universal language. When people hear a drum beat they are attracted to it, so your music should be played aloud to encourage dancing and/or contemplation. This will also attract other aakhu to your altar, which I will explain here shortly. Though music your aakhu may choose to express themselves through you using dance.

- Last but not least you need something to symbolize the rebirth of your aakhu on the other side. Many of our ancestors believed that when they physically died that they were dead until some great awakening, so they are surprise to find that they still exist. Some of our ancestors knew that there was existence after death but had no proof of it because our shamanic traditions were suppressed. So, they need something to reflect upon and help them to understand their new role as an ancestor. This is why you might want to put an image symbolizing resurrection such as an icon of Osar. If you want you can use an image of Jesus. The choice is yours.

- Additional items that can be placed upon the het aakhu are things that your aakhu enjoyed while alive. If your grandmother enjoyed sowing, place before her image a small sewing machine or things that seamstress enjoyed. If your grandpa was a mechanic you might want to get him an old toolbox and so on. This will show that you appreciate them and will help to form a bond so they can intervene in physical affairs on your behalf. For instance, your grandmother can be called upon to help you to sow. Your grandfather can be called upon to help you to hunt, and so on. Now it has come to my attention that you do not want to offer your aakhu items that they enjoyed but they used for destructive purposes. I'm sure that if your

103

aunt smoked cigarettes while she was alive but struggled to overcome her addiction. She wouldn't want you to offer them to her, so keep this in mind. This is why when any liquor is offered it should only be in a small amount because you don't want your aakhu drunk.

To Construct the First Floor of the Het (Spiritual House):

First clean the space and table of physical debris with a good pine scented cleanser. You can in addition to this smudge the intended area with sage or some other strong incense like frankincense. Then take the photos of your deceased relatives such as your grandparents, aunts, uncles, etc. and place them on the bottom floor. Don't put photos of living relatives on the altar either. Only put photos of deceased relatives that you didn't have problem with in life. If you place photos of deceased relatives that you had a problem with, they will cause you grief because in your psyche they will still be irritated. In time you may be inspired to place the photos of other deceased individuals on altar. If so, explain to the aakhu before placing their photo the rules, which is that this is your altar and the space is to be used for empowerment and transformation. Photos of your aakhu placed in silver or gold colored picture frames (which indicate that these spirits have ascended to a higher plane of existence). The photos should only have images of those who have made transition. Never put photos of living people on the altar. You can also have dolls or icons symbolizing your aakhu. Also do not hang your aakhu on the walls of your altar if you can help it.

In some practices it is suggested that you put items symbolizing your ancestors' faith. Based upon my experience, I have learned that this is so that you respect the religious views that they had while alive, but it is not necessary. Because contrary to popular belief, your ancestor's religious beliefs have nothing to do with venerating them. The purpose of venerating your ancestors is to honor their memory and ensure that their legacy is not forgotten because of death.

Once the het aakhu has been built, bless the space in whatever way you feel comfortable. A simple blessing praises the Divine and asks that God blesses your aakhu and chases away all negative entities from your sacred space. Since negative spirits called aapepu are imagined as being snakes or worms. A white painted rooster[24] anointed with a high vibrational oil, such as frankincense and myrrh can also be placed on the space to keep the space spiritual pest clean. Also frankincense and myrrh incense can be burned for the same purpose.

The het is built as a semi three level-step altar because it symbolizes God's power and grace ascending and descending from the pure essence Amun Ra. Amun Ra, remember is not the God but symbolizes the pure and renewing essence of the Divine, which is why the Eyes, ankh, crucifix or star are used to symbolize this moment. The bottom tier (step or shelf) is reserved for the aakhu because they are the closest to us since they are the most recently removed who made transition into KAMTA[25]. Their space is not placed directly on the ground because they are elevated. The ground level is reserved for lower spirits who have not ascended to the aakhu status as of yet. If you are unable to build the altar without placing your aakhu on the floor, simply create a small platform to elevate them a little off of the floor.

The second tier or second floor is left clear because it is your aakhu that will help you to establish a rapport with your netcharu. The idea is similar to being presented to someone of nobility. So you see, the purpose of beginning with your aakhu is so that they can introduce you to the netcharu. When you are ready, your aakhu will guide you to a netcharu, because the aakhu are like representatives or emissaries of the netcharu. The netcharu can be thought of as being like the greatest of our grandparents. The same way it was your parents that introduced you to your grandparents, it is the aakhu that introduce us to the netcharu.

---

[24] Roosters symbolize resurrection.

[25] For this reason, in many Afro-spiritual traditions it is very important that you treat your elders with respect because they are nearing the ancestral state. The last thing you want your elders to remember about you before they made transition into KAMTA is how ill you treated them in their last days on earth. It is because of this cultural understanding many non-Westerners will not put their elderly in nursing homes.

105

The idea is when you stand in front of your altar; you are standing in front of your extended spiritual family. You don't go to your (spiritual) family just to ask for help. You go to your family for all of your needs, therefore offerings and prayers are also addressed to them, so that they can assist us in our life. We basically are their eyes and ears or representatives in the physical. We inform them of what is going on and they offer advice on how to resolve the problem, but they cannot make decisions for us. Their purpose is to provide advice and counsel because they still have ties and influences in the physical communities and in the spiritual realm as well. That being said, do not use your altar as a resting place for miscellaneous items such as your keys, loose change, mail, etc. It is a sacred space and should be respected as such. Everything placed on the altar should either pertain to a ritual or be used for ritual purposes.

In time as you continue to work with your aakhu; they will introduce you to the netcharu. Typically speaking, the netcharu that takes center stage is your principal spirit or the clan that you belong to. This spirit like a totem animal walks with you in the physical and spiritual realm. Though people may identify with different netcharu throughout their lifetime and various circumstances, your clan netcharu will be your primary guardian. So, do not rush this process. Allow your aakhu to introduce you to the netcharu slowly because working with the netcharu is another set of responsibility.

Dealing with Unaccepted Aakhu

It should be noted that our aakhu weren't perfect. Many of them made mistakes and grave errors because of unwise decisions. All of our aakhu seemed to have learned a lot of their lessons by trial and error. Most of them after learning their lesson simply made adjustments, but some of them didn't. These aakhu most likely were not our favorite but we respected them because of their seniority. They were helpful but they were mean son-of-a-guns. These aakhu we may not want to include on our het aakhu as of yet, but know that they are around. Let these aakhu know that they have to work their way up to the het aakhu, which is a place of honor, by amending their wrongdoings. Explain to them that they can do this only by helping you not to make the same

106

mistakes that you have made. A photograph of this aakhu can be placed on the floor next to the het aakhu and slowly at your choosing can be moved on top of your altar. By doing this it helps them to evolve as well as you. For those who have done us wrong see Medicine for Family Curses.

Communicating with Your Aakhu

When you open communication with your aakhu, begin saying a prayer to God on their behalf asking God to bless your aakhu by giving them strength and wisdom to help them to grow. The Lord's Prayer being a general, yet empowering prayer can be used for this purpose.

Afterwards, knock on the altar or on the floor of the altar (if your altar is on near the floor) three times, as if you would knock on the door of a house. Some devotees prefer to have a little bell, but my aakhu don't like this because it makes them feel like they are trained dogs (or some other animal) responding to the sound of a bell. Again, the aakhu should be made to feel as if they are not dead but have just made transition. I never rung the doorbell of my grandparents' house unless I thought they didn't hear me knocking. By this time, the ringing of a doorbell became annoying, as they rushed to answer. I usually knocked and announced that I was here. Ringing the doorbell is for strangers.

Then light a white candle and talk to your aakhu. Tell your aakhu what is on your mind. Ask them for their blessings and help in obtaining and maintaining good health, love, protection and prosperity for you and your family. Then, if you have time, take out a journal and listen. It is for this reason I recommend honoring your aakhu on a day that is most convenience. Traditionally Monday is the day that most people perform this rite in the Caribbean, but Monday is the busiest day of the week, while Saturday for most people is more convenient. Choose whatever day best fits your schedule. Since a proper state of awareness is needed in order to make spiritual contract, being drowsy or intoxicated will hinder your progress and success. For this reason none of these exercises should be conducted if you are on drugs (alcohol, cocaine, marijuana, etc.). When you want to end the meeting, clap your hands three times, while telling them thank you. The clapping of the hands is actually a way of giving praise. (For more details see Appendix A).

How the Aakhu Communicate With Us

There are several ways that your aakhu will communicate back to you and you should note which is the most effective for you. Often they communicate to us through unconscious urges such as déjà vu experiences and flashes of insight. Because we are dealing with KAMTA and it is so close to the sleep state, dreams are the most common ways our aakhu will communicate to us. There are two types of dreams that occur in our regular life. Most of our night dreams are basically a reflection of our past experiences. For instance, if you dream of being at work, this is just your sahu replaying a habit that you are familiar with. This type of dream is basically what is considered psychic noise because it offers no new insight into your life. If however, you dream of being at work and wearing a particular color suit and someone gives you a message that seems very real. If you notice a particular pattern that occurs and the dream unravels into a story. This is most likely a message from your aakhu. Unlike psychic noise dreams, dreams from your aakhu stay with you for a long time because it is like someone was directly in front of you giving you the message.

As you can see, it is very helpful that you keep a journal and write down your dreams and the conversations that you have with your aakhu. Remember, when talking to your aakhu the answer does not have to be anything dramatic or audible. Just follow your intuition and pay attention to your senses. Don't forget. When asking for advice around unresolved issues to always write down the solution that comes to you, but always remain skeptical. Never fully commit yourself to the advice that is given. Always try the spirit to see test their accuracy. Your aakhu will understand why you are doing this.

If you receive a dream from them and you don't like how it plays out. Rewrite the dream by changing the outcome. The way to do this is when you have received the dream. Go into a light trance and simply imagine what it is that you want to occur in the dream. Repeat the image in your mind until it becomes automatic and the original dream meaning was lost. This is very effective when we have nightmares. You can also while dreaming ask your aakhu for help revolving around issues. If the advice is sound and improves your life, then show your appreciation by offering your aakhu, unsalted food.

Feeding and Paying Your Aakhu

When you have petitioned your aakhu for help and you feel that they have come through. You should feed them the foods that they enjoyed in life. The rule however in feeding your aakhu, which you will find exists in all traditions around the world that venerate the dead is to never salt their food. There is no clear explanation as to why spirits don't like salt, but they just don't and if you salt the food. Your aakhu will not be able to absorb the energy offered.

To offer food simply place the food on the plate dedicated for this purpose. I usually find it more convenient to offer the food on the day I honor them. That way when the candle extinguishes itself the food can be removed from the altar before it begins to spoil. In some traditions, the descendants eat the food offered to the aakhu. People that have consumed food that was offered to the aakhu have noted that there appears to be something missing from the food. In other traditions, the food is taken to a remote place in nature and discarded. Since all of these arouse suspicion, I recommend that if you have a garden to start, a compost garden. If you do not have a garden, discard the food in a garbage disposal. If this is not possible, then make the sign of the cross over a garbage can and throw the food away.

In case you are wondering, flowers are also a very popular way of paying your aakhu because they remind them of the beauty of life. While white flowers are the most common offerings that are given, I have found that the aakhu also like brightly colored flowers especially yellow and orange. The thing with flowers is that they quickly show signs of decay, which you do not want on your altar. When flower petals fall all over the altar, they need to be quickly picked up. Picking up 20 or 30 flower petals from around your sacred space and out of the glasses of water can be a bit tedious. It is the only reason I don't recommend it, but if you feel the urge to offer flower by all means do so. Just be sure to keep your het aakhu clean.

Medicine for Family Curses

The only way to overcome abuse is to "forgive and remember", not forget. By forgiving you acknowledge that the abuse was real and that you need to do something to overcome it. By forgiving them you are able to move beyond the abuse but by remembering, you are ensuring that it will never occur again. If you forgive and forget, it causes the abuse to go unnoticed and eventually it will be repeated. One of the ways to accomplish this is a modification of the pebble ritual I gave in the beginning of the book.

Since the aapepu are outcasts in the spiritual realm. What you can do is take something belonging to the abuser. If you cannot find anything then draw a picture or write out on some yellow lined paper (not white) the name of the individual and everything that they have done to you. Let your emotions pour out and be honest. When you have finished take the paper or the item of the abuser, along with a spade or small shovel, somewhere that you don't visit and is not frequented by visitors. Try not to speak or think about anything except for what this individual has done.

When you get to this remote area, dig a hole and tell the individual how you feel. Tell them how they hurt you and how you are better off without them. Take the item belonging to the individual or the paper(s) and forcefully ball it up. Then throw it into the hole, while saying, "You will no longer bother me! I'm finished with you!"

Next bury the item or paper and return back home without looking back and by using a different route. When you arrive home, take a nice bath or shower. Light a white candle asking Osar to cleanse you and put on a dash of Florida Water. Next, do something to get your mind off the ritual indicating that you have moved on like reading a book or watching a comedy. The next day if need be you can begin repairing the damage that was done by getting counseling or therapy.

You can ask your aakhu to also help you to overcome the damage that was done. But understand that it is not your responsibility to help the outcast aapepu to redeem them self. They have to do this them self.

A Final Word of Caution

Because many of the spirits in KAMTA have unfinished business and goals they wanted to achieve in life before their death. It can be a bit overwhelming for you if you have no understanding of spiritual traditions. To get an idea what I mean, imagine going to the grocery store for something you need and all of the people in your house including your neighbors see you are going to the store and give you their shopping list with no money. Most of your aakhu will not take advantage of you in this way, but this is not to say that there aren't those if given the opportunity that will not try. This is why you have to develop your ab – soul through spiritual exercises and strengthen your will. It has to be firmly kept in mind that your relationship with the aakhu is more like a business partnership. You pay them for their services and they pay you for yours. It is an even exchange based upon the principles of Maa. If you ever feel that too many of them are talking and find yourself feeling confused, you can easily dismantle the space. The reason why this happens is because you have attracted some aapepu to your sacred space. By dismantling your het aakhu you are in a way fumigating it. Your true aakhu will understand and need no explanation. At a later date when you don't feel so overwhelmed you can re-erect the space.

Now no one really knows why the aakhu do what they do and why they need certain things; especially without going into trance (which is not encouraged by novices) and dreaming with them. KAMTA is truly a mysterious realm but it believed that the same activities function the same way as they do here in TASETT. For instance, sometimes (well a lot of times) your spirits might want some money. Yes, even though they have no physical body and cannot physically spend it. They may need money. Again why? No one really knows. All you need to know for now is that they do and the faster you accept it, instead of trying to make sense out of it, like I did. The easier you will be able to move along and progress. To offer money, take a

111

dollar bill and rub it vigorously between your hands while thinking of your request and transferring it the money. Then lay it upon the spirits lap (in front of them), but most aakhu will prefer cooked food with no salt.

Most of the aakhu that lived a relatively decent life, after some time in the spiritual realm, begin to understand the nature of KAMTA. The problem that they have is that because our tradition was suppressed, no one is able to enter into a partnership with them to assist them in their objectives. So they might become angry and cause problems in our physical life. Fortunately, most biological aakhu are placated by family reunions and other family events. When they are upset with the direction the family is taking, they are unable to ward off other negative spirits. This is why you should always try to keep them pleased and adhere to their taboos.

The patriarchs and matriarchs of your family lineage created these taboos in order to maintain the family bloodline. These taboos weren't created based upon liberalism but upon practicality. It is because of these taboos you and all of their descendants are alive today. I know about this because as I have recalled in Maa Aankh volume one. I had some cousins that were involved in a very horrible accident because the mother of the family was not following or teaching the ancestral way, which at the time meant attending church. As a result, certain ethical and moral customs were not established. This resulted in negative spirits influencing a greater aspect of their life. It is because of them following their own selfish desires that led to a number of them being imprisoned and killed.

So, if you aren't familiar with your family's taboos just review what is accepted, rejected, what does your entire family consider shameful, embarrassing, disgraceful and honorable. Many of us will find that despite contemporary society's political correctness that our family's views are pretty conservative because our ancestors' beliefs were conservative. This means if you want to change a family tradition, you have to appeal to at least five generations of ancestors in order for it to be accepted. If not, you will be considered an outsider because the concept you are trying to introduce to the family is deemed foreign and thereby detrimental to the survival of the family. If you die as an outsider, your family will give you minimal respect and very little mention, sort of like a dirty secret that no one talks about. This goes for anyone whose actions and behaviors are viewed as being disgraceful, dishonorable and wicked.

If you can convince your aakhu that what you are doing will enhance the lives of your family, help them to survive and is not based upon your selfish desires. Then you will gain their support and will be remembered by the family. If you cannot and you try to implement changes based upon your selfish desires or society's warped view, which your aakhu see as being a deviation. You will be treading on the tail of a tiger without their support.

Remember the aakhu are concerned with political correctness. They are more concerned with ethical and moral living, and getting things right with the Divine, which means helping us to become responsible human beings.

Chapter 6:
Obtaining Power over Evil

The devil from the Kamitic perspective is not a red-skinned boogeyman used to scare children into acting and behaving correctly. The devil or Set is all of our conditionings (addictions, anxieties, etc.) that have been personified. When we study Kamitic history and lore, we find that initially Set was associated with foreigners to Kamit. Most of these foreigners came from the north and were welcomed by the original inhabitants of Kamit. Then somewhere along the line, these foreigners of the land began to fight for control of the throne. After these original inhabitants of Kamit were conquered, defeated, divided through civil strife, reunited, then rebelled and reclaimed the throne of Kamit. Set was forever remembered and associated with chaos, confusion, and disorder caused by an outside influence or external sources. He went from being called Set, to Set-an, then Satan. Later, he became Lucifer and finally the devil.

The idea was not that foreigners are evil but that anything that foreign to our original nature was evil. In other words, our original nature was pure until foreign influences swayed who we are and make us think different. This same model was adopted in Kamitic medicine, whereas harmful bacteria and viruses are also associated with Set. So, we see, Set was not always evil, when we look at the *Story of Osar* in comparison with history. We see that he was a little jealous energy that exists inside of all of us. That manifested into an evil force due to envy, which took over an entire country. Rather than choosing to accomplish his goals in a peaceful and diplomatic way, he chose to resolve his difference through violence. I hope that you can see that the battle between God and the devil is actually a battle between God and us. We become the devil as soon as we decide not to listen to our ba and do whatever it is that we want to do based upon our beliefs and conditionings.

We have to remember that the physical realm functions on a cause and effect basis, which means nothing, happens by coincidences. Behind every effect is a cause, and what you did a few minutes ago or a lifetime ago, is effecting you now. This may be difficult to accept, but the sooner you do. The easier it will be for you to take charge of your life and focus on what you need to do in the present. It may feel good for the moment to have a pity party and complain about everything, but it doesn't make the problems go away by any means. It is only by taking responsibility for your actions and behaviors, instead of blaming others for your shortcomings, that your life gets better and this is one of the key differences between those who listen to their ba and those who follow the impulses of their sahu. We can summarize this into several points.

Children of Osar versus the Casualties of Set

While we are all children of the Most High, there are two types of people in the world. Those who choose to listen to their ba, which we will call Children of Osar, and those that choose to follow their sahu and are victimized by Set. The key difference between the two is that the:

Children of Osar...	*Casualties of Set...*
… Rely upon their five senses and their inner sense to shape their reality.	… Only believe in what they can see, touch, taste, smell and hear.
… Focus on personal empowerment and improving the lives others by raising an individual's consciousness. They know that if you teach an individual how to improve their life, they will go out and help others to do the same.	… Focus on conquering or overpowering others through external means like money, military might, and other power plays. They know no other way of creating change, which is why they always result to threats and violence.
… Live their life as if they are connected to everyone. They do not need to personally know everyone in order to justify treating others with dignity, kindness and respect,	… Live their life as if they are disconnected from everyone and everything. In their mind the world is separated into the haves and the have-nots. Determined

regardless of their association and status.

... Know that they are not alone and that God is everywhere and in everything. Accepting that God is an incomprehensible, unimaginable and indescribable being allows them to have an open mind and learn from everyone and everything. They work with God, so that when help appears to them especially in times of need they know that it is because of synchronicities.

... Believe that while it is important to do your best in any endeavor. Happiness doesn't come from things but from God. Material blessings come into our lives at a much faster rate when we genuinely, focus on helping others, and not taking advantage of them. They focus on being the best only to do the best for others.

... Knows that their greatest ally lies within, so when in doubt and whenever there is

to be a have, they build superficial relationships with people that will help them to achieve their materialistic goals. They treat people based upon the things an individual has.

... Believe in a God and believes that God will judge them based upon how good or bad they were in life. But for the most part, God is a distant being separate from reality that they might see when they die. God is a reference point to fall back upon when things go awry. When help appears in their life, it is seen as an accident, chance or a coincidence

... Believe that the only way to be happy in this world is by doing better than others. Therefore, it is important to always get the best grades, better education, etc. so that you can get the best jobs, the best cars, the best houses, etc.

... The idea of going within, listening to their higher self or ba, seems silly, foolish and any uncertainty. They go within to seek a solution to what troubles them, and allow the Divine to intuitively reveal the solution to them as an intuitive thought. They live their life by faith and knowing.

... Believe that their intuition is actually the way the Divine communicates to them. This makes it more than just a hunch. Understanding that our universe also consists of a spiritual reality and that they are conduits. Makes the Children of Osar rely upon their intuition in all areas of their life, so that the Divine can express Itself through them freely.

... Know that the physical realm is based upon cause and effect, but the spiritual realm is based upon an individual's thoughts. Miracles can be created in our life by simply holding on a specific thought since it is our thoughts that stimulate our actions and behaviors. To create change, they know there has to be a change in consciousness, so they combine natural science with spiritual science.

weird. They prefer to get their solutions by relying on the opinions of others by reading, studying, analyzing and theorizing. They prefer to live their life based upon theory than by following some hunch.

... Believe only in the power of their will and might. As seen from above, they learn the hard way, because as you already know. When you don't follow your intuitive nudges, you end up paying later. Yet the *causalities* prefer to continue living this way and kicking themselves in the butt later for not listening to their intuition and hunches.

... Only believe in what they can see. They do not believe that their thoughts contributed to the state they are in. So, suffering exists because people do evil and the only way to get rid of suffering is by removing evil. But where is evil and how do they find it? No one knows, which is why prison systems are grossly over populated and the problems continue to grow.

... Are conscientious, ethical and respectful because knowing that they are connected to everyone and everything. Makes them appreciate their life but also respect the life of others. So they are not selfish. They do not plunder from other or the planet and worry about the consequences later. They give and share freely when they can, knowing that their needs will be taken care of as well. They look forward to living the memories of others when they physically die and return to the spiritual realm.

... Live only for the now. They talk a good game about how they are concerned about the environment and the future of children, but this is all a ploy. They are only concerned about themselves because they believe they only have one life to live, so they have to get what they want now by any means. Even if it includes harming others and poisoning the environment, so long as they get what they want. Everything is fine, because after all we all are going to die someday. This makes the *Causalities of Set* miserable, grudge holding, vengeful, competitive individuals, only concerned with the bottom line.

Please note that although I have classified people as being *Children of Osar* and others as being *Casualties of Set*, we must not fall into the belief that there are good and bad people. All people are good. Set was not born evil. He just did evil things. He is at the lowest point of his spiritual evolution.

So, when an individual is not living up to their potential, you have to ask yourself. "This is according to whom?" If an individual has chosen to spend their lifetime in pursuit of material things, then that's their prerogative and they should not be criticized or judged. It should just be understood that they simply have not developed the need to change. It must be remembered that we all were once fully controlled by our Set, because none of us were born wise. We were all foolish babes that over a course of time became wiser as life progressed. I say this to say, do not criticize or judge your fellow brothers and sisters. Do not call them ignorant, stupid or fools because they do not share your beliefs or desires. Accept them for who they are and what they are which is Children of Osar even if they do not see the Divine within them. At the same time, if you see someone that is down especially your family or loved one, as a Child of Osar, this is the time to pick them up and give them words of encouragement. Bless those who are hurt, embarrassed, challenged and under the influence of devil.

Now that being said, don't be a fool and become a victim yourself. The same way you had to work to overcome struggle, they have to do the same. The same way you had to develop your consciousness to improve your life. They have to do the same. This is very important that you understand this because if you pity them in their plight you will do them a disservice and yourself as well. You will find that the same boulder chasing them down the mountain is chasing you as well. This means that if you have things like money and food to share, so long as you have enough for yourself do so. Your responsibility is to you and your loved one first and foremost, then everyone else. The whole idea that people have of being selfless is not correct. If you have a dollar and you see someone in need. It is better you both have 50 cent, then they have a dollar and you have nothing. That's what true sharing is all about.

Let me give you an example of what I mean. I remembered when I was going through "the life." I had acquired a substantial amount of debt. When I finally found a secure job, I spent a lot of time paying this debt off. It took me several years to get this debt off, but with self-discipline and determination I got it paid off. I remember I felt so relieved after getting this financial monkey off my back. Then, not too long afterward there were people asking me if they could get a credit card or a car in my name for them. Now, I didn't help these individuals financially. I just told them how I went about doing things. If I had given into their whims these individuals would never had learn how to be responsible for their own finances. They would not have learned how to balance their own checkbooks or how to develop the discipline not to buy everything that glimmers in their eye. This would seem to be commonsense but in our contemporary society it is not because we are all encouraged to give into our ego. Those who don't give into the whims of their ego or the whims of other people's ego are criticize as not being caring or selfish. When you attune yourself to your Osar, you will know when to be charitable and do things for others, and when not. No one will be able to goad and prod you into doing something that you do not want to do. The reason is because your spirit will speak to you and it will be confirmed with by an external act as well.

I have met a number of people who have benefited from this knowledge. I can recall how one of my brothers used this. He told me once that there was this very attractive lady that he knew whom he helped from time to time like helping her carrying groceries into her house, moving furniture, etc. He told me that this lady told him one day that "God said you are the man I need," which he quickly and politely responded, "Well, God didn't tell me that." With that said, he stopped helping this lady so much.

If my brother didn't know anything about his higher spirit, he would have fallen for this ruse. Now, this lady may have been genuine and may not have had any ill intent in mind for my brother. Whatever her intentions were is a perfect example of how most of us get into binds by following the whims of our ego. Our ego or Set remembers makes us pursue instant gratification. It causes us to give into our fears, anxieties, passions, etc. I believe that if more teenagers were taught about their ba – the higher division of their spirit, instead of being taught that if they engage in premarital sex they are going to go to hell. Teenage pregnancy would be greatly reduced. The reason so many teenagers disobey religious authority is because there is no man or woman alive that has a hell to put anyone in, and teenagers know this. The time has come for us to grow up and get real. Suppressing our lower spirit does not work. We need to learn self-control and the only way to do is by listening and working with our Osar.

The Spiritual Wickedness in High Places

The bible states and I paraphrase, "We wrestle not against flesh and blood, but against principalities, against powers, against the rulers of the darkness of this world, against spiritual wickedness in high places." This means there is a war going on and it is not a visible war but a spiritual war. Many of us are familiar with the most common spirits of Set such as the spirit of gossip, the spirit of backbiting, the lying spirit, the spirit of lust, the spirit of infidelity, the cancerous spirit, etc., because these spirits are transferable. Meaning if you are around individuals or places where these spirits dwell, you pick up these spirits and carry them around with you. You know that one of these spirits has attached it self to you because you find yourself at the present moment constantly thinking about them. For most of us, we unknowingly bring these spirits home with us from our workplace, pass by a cemetery, and visit someone in the hospital or even after watching television and seeing a very graphic and disturbing image. Usually most of us recognize these spirits and force them to leave by changing the way we think, act and behave. Some of these spirits like the spirits of various illness however only leave after the whole being has been treated, which consists of taking prescription medication, changing one's diet and so on.

But there are those spirits that empower these lesser spirits. Have you ever wondered why two people can become ill and after treatment they both recover, but then the same ill-ness returns to one of the individuals in the same or different location. After the patient is treated again, the ill-ness returns sometimes with another ill-ness. It is because the spirit empowering the ill-ness' return is what I call one of the conspirators of Set.

Just for the record, I never really believed in spirits because as I mentioned earlier, I was never directly taught about them. When the conversation came up around the grownups, they always talked in code, so as not to let the children know who and what they were talking about. The few times I heard about these entities during my childhood was in church. The first time, I remember is when during church service every now and then a man or woman would wander inside off the street and cause all sorts of ruckus. In those times, the elders and qualified ministers and missionaries would enclose the individual and pray over them to exorcise the spirit. After the spirit was gone, nothing

121

else was ever said about what happened. When we children asked about it, we were simply told that it was a demon and nothing more.

My most memorable childhood experience with these spirits occurred when my brother and I after Sunday morning service came home and after eating lunch began playing on Sunday afternoon. Then suddenly our playing turned to us arguing and fighting with each other as most childhood siblings do. In response, my mother after hearing us bickering would yell, "Get your clothes back on. We are going back to church." and we did. Then she threatened that if we kept up our fighting. She was going to make us sit together on the front pew in order to drive the devil out of us. The funny thing is that we weren't always the only ones sitting on the front pew. Almost any given Sunday evening service you would find children there. Eventually it clicked in our young minds that if we didn't want to go back to church and miss *Animal Kingdom* and the Disney cartoon that came on afterwards. We better hold off our fighting with each other until it is too late to go back to church.

Although I know now that these spirits are classified as being demons, I refuse to call them as such because I believe it would focus attention on an external source. Instead of placing blame where it should be and it is on our actions and behaviors. As I had mentioned, my brother and I weren't the only children on the pew and this was a common remedy to making a child act right. I believe that if people were taught that they are not just innocent bystanders and that these spirits don't just jump us, so we should be afraid of them. People would take more responsibility of their actions and behaviors. These spirits however generally speaking are called in the Kamitic language aapepu, which is any negative, destructive, discouraging spirit known also as haints (hants or haunts).

Aapepu are devilish and demonic spirits commonly known today as ghosts. As I mentioned I prefer not to call these entities demons because most of us have been taught to think that demons are the devil workers that dwell with him in a fiery inferno. We have been shown this image for so long that many of us literally believe in it and totally miss the metaphorical truth, which is that the fire simply symbolizes that an individual is living in anguish because of his and her

122

conscience and lack of evolution. So, the aapepu are described as being vicious and venomous snakes or worms in the afterlife, because they were vicious and venomous acting people in life. Like snakes that prey upon others, as aapepu they continue to do the same in the afterlife.

In the Kongo, the aapepu are called bankyu, which were individuals that engaged in all sorts of negative acts such as adultery, murder, sorcery, theft, etc. They are considered the outcast of society because no one wanted to deal with them and their negative way of life, while they were alive, so the same holds true in death. Just like in life, these lowlifes sat around doing nothing except looking for trouble to get into. In death these lowly spirits are about doing the same thing especially since they live on outskirts of KAMTA and have no permanent residence. When we come in contact with them. We can detect their presence by the discouraging and negative thoughts that disturb our daily affairs.

Now, I can already hear the objections to this perspective, but please note that I am not trying to refute Western medicine nor am I am claiming that ill-nesses are all in our head and do not exist. What I am offering is a different perspective on how we can go about treating from a holistic perspective alongside Western treatment since it tends to only focus on, treating ill-ness as a separate entity based upon its location and response to treatment. As stated in the beginning, the information is not intended to diagnose, prescribe, treat or replace any health disorder whatsoever. Its purpose is strictly educational and it is intended to be used alongside a responsible healthcare program prescribed by an adequate healthcare provider, as an adjunct.

I however discovered while I was trying to recuperate from my ill-ness that when I engaged in certain behaviors and thought patterns I felt worse. For instance, when I complained about having to attend a function that if I really didn't want to go and could not find a way out of the engagement. I suddenly came down with an ill-ness. The ill-ness rather it was a migraine or a recurring rash or the problem, wouldn't go away until I rid myself of the thought pattern and behavior. It took me a while to track these spirits because it requires really investigating and studying your actions and behaviors. It was only after some deep-seated soul searching and research, that I fond that these are the culprits that cause the greatest problems in our life. They are:

The Aapep Spirit of Failure

One of the greatest spirits that our enemy has used against us is our own failure. The way it works is you have decided that you are going to go on a diet to lose 20 pounds or more. So, you go on the diet determined not to eat certain foods. Then later on, you find yourself failing a day or so later. Then you wonder why you failed. Later, when you try to get back on the horse and commit to yourself that you will succeed. You have your past failure haunting and discouraging you.

Well, stop beating yourself up. The reason why you failed is because you didn't properly plan. As we saw earlier in this book, Set encourages us to be reactive and not proactive. Meaning, most of the time people decide they want to go on a diet is because they saw some supermodel or actor, actress on the cover of some magazine promoting some unhealthy product. Instead of thinking, a lot of people react with "I want to look like him or her." Again, without thinking they go and get some diet pills or get on a diet plan and full steam ahead. Then they lose their way because they are either restricting the wrong foods from their diet or not getting the nutritious foods that they should be consuming. As you know because we have all been here before, they end up spending all sorts of money on exercise equipment or the like, but the objective is never achieved.

Defense against the Aapep Spirit of Failure

The way this spirit works is by deceiving you due to your lack of knowledge and understanding. Set's largest group of casualties is those who don't even know they have been duped, because Set loves taking advantage of peoples' ignorance. He actually has people believing that all they have to do is pray and magically or miraculously they will be healed of illness, shed excessive weight, and cured of poverty, etc. without changing themselves, if it were only that easy. It would be great, but that is not how the universe functions.

124

The simplest way to plan is to:

1. Know that if other people have accomplished a similar goal you can accomplish it as well, but in order to achieve it. It will require that you give the same kind of commitment and determination. You can't expect to be a doctor if you only study or work at it for a couple of hours out of the week. You can't expect to be millionaire if you aren't devoted to learning how real millionaires invest in helping others. You can't expect to lose weight if you aren't willing to change your dietary lifestyle.
2. Ask yourself if this is really what you want in your life. This is the number one reason why people fail to achieve what they want because they don't know what they want out of life.
3. After this has been established list your likes and dislikes in regards to the goal. Describe if possible how to achieve your goal. The purpose of doing this is so that you don't fool yourself. It will help you to see what you need to do. Once you begin to see the skills you don't have developed, you can begin to work towards developing them.
4. Create an image of what you want or where you want to be. If you are a student and you want to be a teacher. You would imagine yourself teaching a class full of young minds with eloquence and poise, as having complete control, respect and knowledge. You would imagine being a teacher in various situations and continue to grow this seed in your mind until it becomes habitual. Contemplate on this image as much as you can especially during your times of leisure. The image should become automatic so that whenever a feeling of doubt comes about, it pops into your awareness and keeps you motivated towards your goal.
5. If you fall off the track, simply get back on your plan. Don't let anyone or anything deter you from what you feel that you want to be.

If you follow these five steps, the Divine's Power – Rau – will support you in achieving your goals. You can use these same steps planning to get whatever you want. Make sure that when you have achieved a goal that you make a new plan.

Another important point that I must mention is that when you think from this perspective. You must rid yourself of the belief that you are in competition with others. This is a ruse created by Set, which if you recall motivates us to act and behave based upon our physical limitations and resources. As a Child of Osar you must think from a creative perspective and not a competitive. One of the reasons for doing this besides the fact that it gives you access to unlimited resources. Is that by thinking from a competitive perspective you are in essence cursing what you want, that others have. This is twisted form of envy. For instance, if I owned a jewelry store and across the street from my store is a similar jewelry store, that appeared to be very successful. If I conduct my business by trying to compete with them, what is motivating me? I am trying to get more customers, if not take the other store's customers, because I want to be more successful and I want the other business to fail. Can you see the selfishness in competing with one another and how quickly envy rears its head? The reason the other store is successful is because they have learned that there is a certain way to do things. Instead of competing, I need to learn what I need to do in order to improve my jewelry business.

When you compete for something that another has, it is like taking the quick road to success. It is like if you wanted to be a physician, instead of going through the proper training to be a doctor. You skipped all of that and just focused on wearing medical apparel. As a result, no one respects you and you can't respect yourself because you know that you are not properly prepared. So don't compete, instead try to understand what made your "competitor" successful and try to do the same thing that made them successful.

The Aapep Spirit of Laziness and Procrastination

We've all been here before as well, the moments where we just don't want to do anything. It can be something as simple as taking out the garbage to helping an individual in need, but instead of moving when we should. We lollygag around and wait until the last minute to take care of business. If you will recall from the beginning of the book the reason people don't have what they want. It is because of this weapon. This weapon has altered more lives because when people wait to the

126

last minute to do something. It has a ripple effect resulting in us rushing and becoming impatient. When we rush there is a strong tendency for us to cause mishaps. Just think about the driver who is late to work going 45 mph in a school zone. Then when this individual gets a ticket they want to fault the cop, the school zone and even the alarm clock, when in actuality blame lies with them. Now, there are some times when you can't prevent being late like having a flat tire, but 95% of the time we can if we just listen to that voice speaking within.

The voice within, our Osar, gives us hints all of the time that we should heed to. You can be walking to your car one day and your attention is drawn to your tire. It comes to you intuitively that you need to put air in the tire or someone mentions that you need to check it out. When you get intuitive advice like this you need to act on it now. There are numerous stories that have been recorded of individuals getting an idea and responding instantly, which improved their health, brought them a fortune and even saved their life.

Defense against the Aapep Spirit of Laziness and Procrastination:

When you receive an idea to do something that is constructive and will minimize arguments, chaos and confusions. Do it and don't delay. Even if you aren't sure what the outcome is, for instance a thought comes to pray for someone that is ill. Do it, send blessings to that individual the best way you can. Don't give in to laziness and procrastination. Don't delay.

The Aapep Spirit of Arrogance

In this competitive world it is easy to be attacked by this spirit, especially if you come from a less than privilege background. It plays out like this; you are attending your high school reunion. Then you see some people that always thought they were better than you. You listen to them talk about all of the things that they have done and the places they have been. You have accomplished a number of fantastic goals yourself and you want to rub it in their snobbish face. You feel the

127

pressure mounting and feel that like you are ready to explode. This is
the Arrogance Bomb that has started ticking. If this bomb goes off you
are going to go off as well and make a fool of yourself, which is what Set
wants.

Defense against the Aapep Spirit of Arrogance:

Don't do it! Just ignore the temptation and if you need be don't say
anything. This is one of those tests that if you learn to be quiet and
resist the urge to brag about your self; it will pay off in the end. I
remember facing a similar situation and after passing the test. An
observer watching the whole thing came up to me and struck up a
conversation, which led to me getting some very useful information. If I
had followed my impulses, I am sure that the destructive behavior
would have made him leave to avoid getting caught up in the
confrontation.

The Aapep Inverted Spirit of Arrogance

This spirit like the previous one appears when we feel pressure to act
just to impress others. This spirit causes us to act, dress, talk, etc. based
upon how we think others will perceive us. Stop worrying about what
others think of you. If you don't understand something, it is best to say
that you understand a subject. Than it is to try and to explain a subject
you don't comprehend. We need to break this habit and prevent this
self-sabotaging weapon from going off, by not lying.

The inverted spirit of arrogance also appears in the form of self-
pity by making you believe that you can't achieve the same thing that
another has done. It makes you feel worthless and if you feel like
nothing then you feel like you have nothing to lose. Don't fall for this
trick.

Defense against the Aapep Spirit of Inverted Arrogance:

If you are guilty of this you are basically lying to yourself, which is
preventing you from achieving any objective you have at hand. When
you lie to yourself because you are worried about what others think.

You do yourself a disservice by cutting yourself off from individuals that could help you.

The Aapep Spirit of Excessive Pride

Boasting is another form of arrogance. When you boast about your accomplishments, you are basically telling people that you are better than them. This spirit has the tendency to separate you from others. Besides making people envious of you, it presents you as a show off. Now, there's nothing wrong with being proud that you accomplished or fulfilled a goal. The problem comes when all you can think about and talk about is how you achieved that goal.

Defense against the Aapep Spirit of Excessive Pride:

Don't let Set give you a big head, because when you begin thinking, "Look what I have done," you've disconnected yourself from the Rau. When you switch to this way of thinking you begin using your art, talents and skills to determine what you can get. You easily lose sight of the original intention and purpose of your objective. For instance, if you are an artist you begin creating artwork to see how much money you can get, instead of creating artwork because you enjoy it. One way to prevent yourself from boasting is to look at other projects that you can complete.

The Aapep Spirit of Attachment and Control

We all come from different backgrounds and we have different experiences, which have shaped our belief. As a result, everyone is not going to agree on how to complete a task. So when someone offers constructive criticism on how to complete the task from his or her perspective. Don't think that your way is right and their way is wrong or vice versa. Look at it from a cause and effect perspective.

Far too often, when someone tells us that the way we are completing a task will yield minimum results. We get offended and assume that they are attacking us, are beliefs, our way of life, etc. Learn how not to take things to heart. When someone offers constructive criticism be willing to see it from his or her perspective and don't be afraid to change.

Defense against Aapep Spirit of Attachment and Control:

We should always remember that nothing in the physical world is permanent. Everything in the physical realm will soon cease to exist and pass, which means instead of focusing on trying to keep things in our life. We should be focusing on maintaining our peace and happiness when these things are no longer present. We have to learn how not to stake our peace and happiness to money, our relationships, jobs, careers, cars and homes. Yes, these things are important and we need them to physically survive, but learn how to be happy if you have them or not.

This also applies to individuals in relationships, where the husband is so attached to his wife, that he will not let her do anything outside of his control. There are also women in this same situation, where they don't trust their husbands, so they figure they must keep a tab of him and everywhere he goes. The fear of loss and envy driving these individuals that they must control their spouses is the preparing them for their downfall. Woman and man were not created to be slaves to anyone. We created to express the Divine's Will, so whenever we are in these situations. There is a growing part within us that yearns to be free, which is our soul. Soon or later our ab soul will revolt, which is why Hru continued to challenge Set.

So, we have to learn that true love is not attachment and control. Yes, it hurts when someone we care about leaves, but we have to remind ourselves that this is our sahu's way of responding to loss. Spiritually speaking no one ever leaves out of our life. We still have very strong memories of these individuals because we are all connected. Remember, that Set challenges us so that we can see our divinity, which means that if you are in this situation. It is because your objective is to learn that the only one you are supposed to depend upon is the Divine within for your peace and happiness.

130

The Aapep Spirit of Guilt

There is nothing worse than carrying around the feeling of guilt and shame when you have done something wrong. The purpose of guilt and shame is to make us feel remorseful about incorrect actions and behaviors. It was not intended for us to carry this burden around for rest of our days on the planet. This is one of Set's most effective ways of disconnecting us from the Rau. Usually when he attacks us with this weapon it always has something to do with the past.

Defense against the Aapep Spirit of Guilt:

Combat Set with the fact that when you committed wrong it was because you didn't know any better. You were younger and you didn't know what you know now. Don't let the Enemy make you feel bad because of something you did in the past. Let it go and know that because you no better now you can make a positive change today. The next time when a similar event comes up, step up and do what you know is the righteous thing to do.

The Aapep Spirit of Hopelessness

It is hard to have faith especially when we are taught in this world that 'seeing is believing', but we must have faith and the way to increase your faith is by knowing. When you put a light bulb in a socket, provided the electric bill is paid, you don't believe that the lights will come on when you flip the switch. You have a knowing that they will because time and time again. After putting a light bulb in the socket and flipping the switch the lights have come on. You basically expect the lights to come on all of the time provided you follow this same procedure. You have faith.

Defense against the Aapep Spirit of Hopelessness:

The Enemy knows that because we cannot physically see the spiritual realm that surrounds us that it is easy to lose faith. He therefore sends the spirit of discouragement to accompany our growing lack of faith.

The only way to resist this weapon is like constantly putting a light bulb in the socket. You have to practice and practice, which will build up your confidence and faith. Whenever you lack confidence and faith in your abilities, it is because you aren't sure of yourself. The only way to become sure is to try it out.

The same approach can be applied to spiritual matters as well. If we believe that God is All-knowing, then God knows if we lack faith in the Divine. How then do you increase your faith in God? It is by trying God. It is the only way we can truly know something, which is why it is always advised not to believe anything that someone tells you without trying it out for yourself.

The Aapep Spirit of "What If"

We've all done it some time in our life. We've allowed Set to talked us out of getting a promotion, meeting that special someone, advancing in life, etc. all because we thought, "What if…" The "What If…" spirit is a weapon based upon our fear of the future and fear of the unknown. It is because can't see beyond our garments. We always question what will happen if we take a certain course of action, because we don't want to lose the things that we have acquired and obtained. The interesting thing about "what if…" scenarios, is that usually 90% of the time, the "what if…" scenario never takes place.

Defense against Aapep Spirit of "What If"

Don't let Set unleash the "What if…" spirit on you. Instead of thinking "What if…" fill in the blank with something affirmative. For instance, you are querying about a job promotion instead of "what if I don't get this job?" Think, "What if they like the fact I am interested in this position?" For better health, "What if the physician gives me a clean bill of health?" and so on. Remember the only way to rid yourself of fear is by doing what you are afraid of. By thinking something better is coming you are change the outcome.

The Aapep Spirit of Humiliation

No one likes being embarrassed and humiliated because it makes you feel like you are silly, vulnerable or worst a fool. So when most people get into an embarrassing situation, their immediate response is to try to cover it up or act like it never happened. This spirit in turns causes people to lie and after you tell one lie. Then you have to tell another in order to cover up the previous lie that was told. What's worse is that eventually the truth ends up making it known.

Defense against the Aapep Spirit of Humiliation:

Don't allow yourself to be overtaken by this spirit. When an embarrassing situation occurs, breathe calmly and acknowledge it for what it is, and then move on. Don't lie and try to cover it up, that's what Set wants you to do, to take the easy route. No, take a proactive stance, by recognizing the cause and effects of the situation. Honesty goes a long way versus lying and being dishonest.

The Aapep Spirit of Doubt and Hesitation

The Enemy has been successful in convincing the vast majority of us that our progress and success depends upon the approval of others. This spirit is so evasive that a lot of times we don't even know that we have succumbed to it because we believe that every time we do something. We need the opinion of others to validate our actions and behaviors. This is why whenever we do something, the first thing we do afterwards is ask what our family, friends or coworkers thinks about the course of action we have taken. The constant dependency upon those who are closest to us prevents us connecting to the God's Rau and makes us reactive to their responses. When you take a proactive stance in life, you do not have to look to those closest to you to validate your actions and behaviors. This is because by being proactive you become the cause instead of the effect. Remember, when you are being proactive, you are acting out of purpose and this is what drives you. If you are just reacting then it is very easy for you to get caught up in the outcome and the opinions of others.

Defense against the Aapep Spirit of Doubt and Hesitation:

Live your life by being proactive and with purpose. When doing a project, don't become discouraged when the results you desire don't manifest. Don't give up and throw in the towel and declare yourself a loser. Take a proactive perspective and remind yourself of the purpose of the project. Reconnect back to the Rau so that you can new ways of achieving your purpose.

The Evil Eye Aapep Spirit

Yes, that's right. The Evil Eye is a very powerful spiritual weapon of Set. It is one of the most frequently unleashed spirits also known as *Mal de Ojo* and *Malochia*. Part of the reason why it is so powerful is because unlike the other weapons (or spirits mentioned above), most people don't believe that the evil eye exists, but it is spoken about all throughout the world, even in Christendom. In fact, in Mark 11:12-14, the apostle tells a story of how Jesus cursed a fig tree for not bearing fruit of season. Afterwards, the tree "dried up from the roots," withered and died. Most people are aware of it but the same energy that Jesus used to cast upon the fig tree is the same way the evil eye works.

There's a couple of reason why the evil eye is so widespread. For one it derives its power mainly from envy. Envy as we have already discussed is a feeling of discontent and a resentful emotion aroused when an individual lacks a possession, qualities or achievement that another possesses. So when someone is envious of you or your belongings. Through their eyes they cast a jealous stare of resentment usually accompany with either a good or ill intended phrase. When this negative energy attaches itself to you, it has the ability to alter your health, ruin your luck and affect every aspect of your life. As I stated earlier, part of its success stems from the fact that Set will tell you that the Evil Eye does not exist and that it is superstitious nonsense. But, all of the great spiritual masters of the world have advised that the pious take caution against it. The only reason why most of us don't believe in it is because Set the master of trickery and deception has hidden the truth from us. He takes great joy in the fact that for some of us, in order for us to accept a truth we have to "see it." But we must remember that TASETT – the physical world is full of illusions. Simply trust you intuition.

The second reason the Evil Eye is so prevalent is because we don't call it the Evil Eye. It is masked, disguised and dressed up to sound pretty, and we refer to it as constructive criticism. Anyone that has ever received constructive criticism will tell you that it didn't sound constructive at all. It sounded like harsh and vile words because they were really the opinions of another. Sincere criticism encourages people to do better through suggestions, not encourage them out of spite and vengeance. If you tell someone that they are fat, ugly, stupid, etc. all it does is make the individual angry because the sahu remember, doesn't distinguish between good or bad, right or wrong, fictional and non-fictional. The sahu takes everything literally, so these words sting and causes it to react and defend itself in whatever way it has learned how. This is when Set steps in and some people respond when they get angry by attacking others, while some people respond by internalizing the harmful words because they lacked the ability to physically defend themselves when they were younger. Consequently, these individuals may find comfort in food, alcohol or some other destructive behavior.

Defense against Harmful Words and Verbal Curses

When you hear harmful words, they are an attack on your personality but not an attack on you, because the individual that issued the verbal attack does not know what you are capable of. They only see what you have accomplished thus far, so don't take what someone tells you to heart. I know this is easier said than done, which is why when someone issues a vile attack on you. Place your right hand over your heart and speak a blessing over yourself to counter the attack. Say the blessing as many times as you have to erase the curse from settling into your sahu. For instance, if someone says, "You're ugly" You need to come back and tell your sahu, "You are beautiful because you are made in the image of the Divine" and repeat it until the hurt goes away. If the individual issues a verbal attack to a child or loved one, if you can place your right hand, over their heart and say a blessing. If you cannot do this simply speak the blessing aloud or silently and direct the blessing to

137

them. If they say something vile about something that you have done or something you possess. Speak the blessing over it and cancel it out.

When you need to sincerely criticize an individual in order to get them to complete a task more efficiently, it is best to do so by making suggestions, so as not to offend the individual. For instance, instead of telling someone that what he or she is wearing is ugly, it may be more productive if you were to say, "You might want to wear something that compliments or is more appropriate." It may sounds like you are sugarcoating, but if you're sincerely trying to help the individual and not tear down. They will appreciate your suggestion.

Now, another interesting thing about the Evil Eye is that most people who cast it don't even know that they are casting it. That's right, it is often cast upon people unintentionally and usually from those who are closest to us. The reason is because we all have a set of beliefs and ideas of what we believe are right and wrong, based upon our upbringing. When we criticize another for something that they have or have done based upon our beliefs. We have in essence just sabotaged ourselves as well because we have condemned ourselves from having the same thing that another has. This is why it is often advised not to curse what another has that you also desire.

For instance, if someone wins a million dollars, if you say, "Why did they win a million dollars? They don't deserve it, or anything negative about their winnings. You have just sabotaged your chances of ever winning a million dollars as well. Instead bless those who have been blessed, so that you can be blessed as well.

It would be great if everyone lived his or her life like this but the reality is that we are not there yet. If you are successful in any of your endeavors, the sad truth is that there are a number of people who are envious of you. They are not happy about your progress or your success, and if they are they still wonder how in the world you advanced when they didn't. The surprising thing is that even after learning about this you still will judge and criticize others whom you feel are unworthy as well, because this negative behavior is hardwired into our sahu. As a result, the Evil Eye has the ability to cause physiological ailment such as frequent dull headaches, fatigue, a general feeling of disability and lack of energy, accompanied with eyestrain. The Evil Eye has been said to be the cause of accidents and slight injuries. In some regions where this belief persists, it is not uncommon to hear of a wife casting the eye on her husband out of resentment, which usually occurs deliberately. So you see it takes a lot of work to purify our soul of this energy.

Other Defenses against the Evil Eye Aapep Spirit:

There are a number of ways to protect against the Evil Eye. Some of the most common preventive measures that can be used to prevent the passing of this negative energy are to give with your right hand and receive with your left hand. Meaning when someone gives you something, try to receive it using your left hand.

The Figa Hand Gesture

Figure 15: Figa (fee-gah) Hand Gesture for Averting Evil Eye

When you catch someone transmitting the Evil Eye, you can averted it by making the sign of the *figa*, (fee-gah) symbolizing catching the evil being caught before it spreads. This hand gesture does not have to obvious but I have noticed that when this gesture is made. It does seem to break the maleficent gaze of the transmitter.

139

Protective Jewelry (Amulets or Bodyguards)

We can also avert the Evil Eye by blocking the certain parts of our body from the eye's influence. Since our ears are constantly receiving messages. To cleanse our ears of spiritual dirt, take a cotton swab soaked in ordinary hydrogen peroxide and clean around the ears every day. Another precautionary method that women may be very fond of is the wearing of jewelry. Earrings were worn specifically for averting the Evil Eye's influence and the spirit of gossip. Other popular jewelry items that were worn to avert this influence were bangles, bracelets and ankle bracelets often with little charms. The most common charms used in Kamit were the ankh but you can use any charm that you believe will ward of the Evil Eye. To charge your charms, see the exercise that follows.

Protective Fragrances

While we need a certain amount of stress in order to live and move through the world. Excessive amounts of stress prevent us from relaxing, healing and being rejuvenated. When stress builds up between our upper shoulders and the back of our neck, it can also make us susceptible to the Evil Eye. A quick and simple remedy to relieve this tension is to take a cool shower. This is a good practice to get in the habit of doing when you come home from work, before interacting with your family, but when you can't take a cool shower. Take a teaspoon of dried basil and put it inside a bottle of Florida Water. If you can't find any Florida Water you can use a regular bottle of rubbing alcohol or a bottle of rum. When you need to use the mixture, sprinkle a little bit on a small cloth and rubbed on your neck. Lemon peels steeped in alcohol can also be used for this purpose. Another option that I know some people would do is to take basil leaves and add it to their favorite cologne and perfume along with some of their essence (saliva or urine) to personalize the charm.

140

Protective Plants

Another way to defend against the Evil Eye is through the use of common day houseplants. This may seem odd to you but you must remember as a Child of Osar we don't just pick up things and place them on our body, in our homes and around our workplace just for aesthetic purposes. When you see the Divine's Rau in everything, this is when you see the beauty of God. To use plants to protect against negative influences. Plant plants with sharp edges and thorns in your home. The analogy is that the plant absorbs the negative influence and disperses it, hence the more negativity it absorbs the larger it grows. Of course, you need to care of the plants as normal, but thank it for the exchange. Some of the most common protective plants used against negative spirits are:

- Aloe prevents against household accidents. It can also be used as a topical ointment for burns, insect bites, ulcers and stings.

- Cactus is another household plant that is often overlooked.

- Pineapple plant – this is the top of the pineapple fruit that is allowed to spout and then planted. When it grows the blades of the pineapple tops grow thick and long.

- Basil is a commonly planted herb for culinary and spiritual purposes. Caring for basil is a little tricky but once you know how it brings peace to the home it is in.

Protective Pets

Since animals do not have an ab – soul as we do, they are more susceptible to negative influences than we are. Goldfish for instance attract good luck, which is why they are so loved in Chinese feng shui and Indian vastu, but goldfish serve a dual purpose. When in comes to the Evil Eye, goldfish especially amongst poorer East Indians is used like a canary in a coal mind. When the fish dies thank it and replace it with another. Some other pets that can serve this same purpose are parakeets.

141

Dogs are loyal animals and have a unique ability to detect negative influences. The great thing about dogs is that they are loyal and most will give you unconditional love.

Miscellaneous Charms

Any sharp object can be used as a charm against negative influences. You can take broken glass, straight pins, and thorns, quills, which can be put into a red glass bottle. This can be then placed on the windowsill and in the corner of one's dwelling near the door. The symbol of an erect phallus can even be used against negative female spirits, as well as warrior statues, since they both symbolize aggression. To purify see the exercise below.

To Remove the Evil Eye Influence:

To remove this influence one of the best ways I have found is to be spiritually cleansed with an egg called a *limpia* (Spanish for cleansing). The analogy is that the egg symbolizes the universe in shape and represents the beginning of life. Since life has not begun signified by its unbroken shell, it is the perfect symbol of purity and can absorb most negativity. There are numerous ways to perform this cleansing but the method I learned comes from my *abuela* (grandmother) who was a *curandera*, a female Hispanic shaman dedicated to treating physical and/or spiritual illnesses.

To perform the limpia take the egg and let it reach room temperature. The egg should be cool not cold. Next while praying and telling the egg to remove all forms of negativity from the individual. Rub the egg starting at the head down towards the feet as if you are sweeping. If you feel the need to rub the egg in certain areas like the eyes, around the chest region or the stomach do so. Always, remember to follow your intuition.

Afterwards crack the egg open and empty it into a clear glass of water or white bowl with water. Take one of the straws from a broom

142

and cut it using scissors into eight pieces. Next make four crosses with the cut straw and situate them around the yoke of the egg, each symbolizing the four directions. Don't worry, if the crosses aren't perfectly placed; just try to place them as best you can. Then place the glass or bowl of water with the egg under the client's bed while they sleep. The next morning if you choose to, observe the egg to see if there has been any change to the egg. Next empty the bowl of water and the egg into the toilet. Then rinse the bowl with salt water and empty it into the toilet.

Exercise 6:
How to Create a Pschent Talisman

Another form of protection is to create a Pschent herst, which is a spiritual necklace for blessings and protection. The Pschent you will recall consist of the red Deshret crown of TASETT and the white Hedjet crown of KAMTA. The reason for creating and wearing these necklaces is because the color red, besides symbolizing TASETT is also the color of blood, caution, aggression and heat. On the color spectrum, the color red has the lowest frequency and therefore, the highest amount of negativity. The color white on the other hand has the highest frequency on the color spectrum and therefore the highest amount of positivity. It is the color of purity, blessings, wisdom, patience, knowledge and coolness. By wearing the white and red necklaces together, we are creating balance and figuratively uniting our kingdoms as the legend of Osar indicates, by forcing our Set to work in our favor and with Osar.

The theory behind this is similar to how vaccines are created by integrating a strain of the actual disease into the serum. The white necklace therefore weakens the negativity of the red necklace; thereby negating the influences directed your way.

How to Activate the Herst

As you may have already guessed, the white and red necklaces resemble the white and red Pschent crown of Hru. This is because we must remember that even though Set is our enemy, we cannot progress without him. Set it must be remembered is our greatest adversary but without him we would not grow nor would we become stronger spiritually and physically. It is Set's resistance to our will that makes us stronger and helps us to survive physically.

At the same time, if we only had the white crown although we may have patience, knowledge and spiritual wisdom. Without the red crown, we may be flighty and not grounded in physical reality like so many "spiritual people" who have high ideals but a weak physical

144

constitution due to poor health, lack of money, etc. So, the two necklaces complement each other. They remind us of the importance of balance, the need to be aggressive but at the same time humble. The red necklace allows the fire to rise to our head but the white cools this fire so that it doesn't consume us, and so on.

If you want to make the herst from hand get a spool of white cotton or wool twine, which is natural and absorbent. Cut the two 20 inch lengths of twine. String the white beads on twine making sure that they don't slide off the other end. Add enough beads so that on both ends you have about an inch of free space remaining. Add a crimp bead to tie the other ends, while cutting off the excess. Then follow the same instructions for the red beads. Of course, if you don't have time to make your herst by hand, you can purchase an all-white and all red beaded necklace from a spiritual supply store.

One of the most powerful ways to empower and activate your herst is to baptize them. First you take a white bowl and put your herst inside. Next, add to it some of your favorite cologne or perfume, Florida Water and a small amount of your personal essence[26] such as saliva and rum by spraying the rum from your mouth into the bowl three times. Then using your middle finger, stir the mixture and your herst counter-clockwise, while telling the waters to empower your herst and protect you from all forms of evil. Then light a cigar, take three puffs and breathe life into your herst by blowing it directly over the herst and mixture. Now, take a small white candle, place it on a saucer and next to the bowl, and then light it. Make sure the candle is not near any flammable objects. When the candle has extinguished itself, the herst is ready to be worn.

Caring for Your Herst

The way the herst works is simple. When someone wishes you ill and they approach you with it. They will get an impression not to bother you. For instance, I saw an individual one time that went to hug me all

---

[26] Personal essence such as saliva and urine are used to personalize charms since each is distinctive to each individual.

of a sudden have a change of heart as if someone told them "You better not!" Then they decided to simply keep their distance and speak instead. I didn't know why they did it. I took a shower, so I know I was clean. The only thing I could think of was that I was wearing my herst.

So the way to care for them is wear them under your clothes. Do not wear them while taking a bath or shower. Also, unless you are doing ritual work, avoid wearing them during sexual intercourse. If someone happens to see them, simply tell them that they are for good luck. Only if they are interested in such matters should you divulge the true meaning of your herst. Your herst is a spiritual tool so it should be treated as such and not thrown around haphazardly. If the herst falls to the floor, it is a sign that it has absorbed its share of negativity and needs to be refreshed using the ritual described above. If the herst breaks it signifies that is absorbed the evil influence directed at you and broke off the attack. It basically has fulfilled its purpose.

When you are wearing your herst, try to be humble and try not to boast too much about your success. Remember, it is the flashiness of your success sometimes that attracts the envious gaze of others. Now don't be modest because it is the right thing to do. Be modest because it serves your purpose and is a preventive remedy against envy. When not wearing the herst, place in a blue or red cloth bag.

Additional Charms

In many shamanistic cultures it is customary to add additional charms and other objects to their costumes especially after a ritual to for additional spiritual power and to illustrate spiritual merit. These charms called *milagros* (miracles) in Spanish contrary to popular opinion are not magical in nature. The only power they have is the power you imbue in it, because they are symbolic of a desired goal and/or a goal achieved by working with one's ba – higher spirit. The Kamitic people were known for wearing a host of charms for fertility, safe pregnancy, and protection against evil and so on. In these contemporary times, you can add these charms to your herst to be used against illness, pain, trouble, for saving a marriage, to improve finances, grades in school, etc., or they can be carried in your pocket, purse or billfold.

146

The most popular charms that can be added to your herst are the Eye of Ra (for added protection against the Evil Eye), the ankh cross (for vitality), a crucifix (symbolizing the maa aankh, hence rebirth), bull horn (strength, vitality), the figa (against all forms of evil), birthstone, folded scriptures or prayers placed in charms, etc. Any symbol that you feel you have a connection to can be added to your herst, because this is the key to using charms. For instance, if the popular valentine heart means a heart to you, use it instead of trying to force another symbol to represent a heart.

Again, you can sense when you may need to put a charm on your herst. For instance, as I was writing this, I found a shark tooth that I bought several years ago in his original packaging. Since I found him, I have had the idea to put him on my herst, which I finally did.

To activate your charm, before placing it on your herst or carrying it. Simply place it in your right hand and sprinkle your favorite cologne, Florida Water in your palm. Then spit three times to add your essence. Next, clasps your hands together to simulate lightning and rub your hands together vigorously, while imbuing the charm with power and thanking it for assisting you on your journey. This does not have to be dramatic. You are simply giving it life and purpose. When you are finished and sense that it is ready to work for you. Add the charm to your herst. If however, you are unable to do this rite for any reason, follow the previous instructions given for activating your herst.

Below is a list of common charms you might be interested in adding to your herst, carrying on your person or placing around your home or place of business:

- Acorn – attracts the opposite gender, increases income, divinatory powers, and prosperity.

- Agate – is for good luck, health, meditation, protection and purification.

- Alligator Teeth – are good for protection from danger and the ill intent of others.

- Akuba – Akan fertility charm used to symbolize one's desired child. Charm can be given the desired name of the child and worn as a keepsake.

- Amber – good for balance, harmony, protection and the psychic (prophetic) development.

- Amethyst – worn to increase intelligence, luck, power, peace, protection, spirituality, psychic development and to find love.

- Ankh – worn to symbolize circle of life and promote good health and rebirth.

- Arrowhead – are carried for protection against enemies, bad luck, hexes, the evil eye and all negative forces. Placed near the front door to prevent burglars from breaking into your home. Placed in your car it helps guard against accidents and theft.

- Arm – body part can be worn to represent the recovery of a condition associated with it the arm, hand or finger, such as an injury, or arthritis. It can also be used to represent ones strength and willingness to work.

- Baboon (or Monkey) – called Aan, sacred ape of Djahuti (Tehuti or Thoth in Greek) carried or worn to mimic (shape shift) and help one learn a skill or talent from another.

- Bear Claw – worn to give one the physical strength of a bear. If claws are worn or carried they have to be obtained ethically and legally in order to be effective.

- Bells – were used as the alert and announce an individual's presence. The sound was used to dispel hostile spirits, ward off the evil eye and attract happiness. In contemporary times, bells have been replaced with bangles bracelets and are worn by women and female children.

- Bennu (Phoenix) – worn to symbolize rebirth and the return of one's health, status, success, etc.

- Books – as well as symbols of notepads and pencils worn to assist students in mastering subjects.

- Bulls – are worn to increase the virility in men. Can be placed under one's pillow or under the bed before sexual intercourse.

- Bull Horns – worn to protect against all maledictions.

- Cat – worn for luck, obtaining secret wishes, prophecy and protections.

- Coins – worn to attract money and deter the evil eye. When new brides wear several coins as wrist or ankle bracelets, they attract family prosperity.

- Cowries – once used as a form of currency are worn to attract fertility, luck, money and prosperity.

- Cows – worn to increase fertility in women.

- Cross – symbolizes the cycle of life (maa aankh) and is worn to ensure that one's soul continues to evolve and is reborn.

- Diamonds – worn for happiness, love and to promote fidelity amongst spouses.

- Dogs – symbolize loyalty and protection.

- Dolphin – are worn to protect the wearer from accidents when traveling by ship.

- Dove – are worn for hope, to bring peace and protection from death, fire and lightning.

- Ducks – are associated with Nebhet (Hthru, Het-Heru, Nephthys in Greek). Due to the saying, "Water off a duck's back," a reference to duck's oily feathers. Ducks symbolize sustained happiness, eternal joy and a loving couple's determination to weather the storm. They can also be used to symbolize progress; hence the saying "ducks in a row."

- Eye of Ra – used to counteract the evil eye.

- Eye of Hru (Horus) – worn for strength, vitality, and protection against the evil eye.

- Figa (fee-gah) – is worn by many Brazilians to avert the evil eye, improves one's luck, prosperity and increase a man's virility.

- Fish – symbolize fertility and male virility. Also can be worn to attract prosperity and increase psychic abilities.

- Foot – can be used to symbolize travel and messages that come by foot. Also can be worn by athletes to symbolize quickness and speed.

- Fox – carried or worn to mimic (shape shift) and help one learn a skill or talent from another.

- Frog – good for increasing fertility and virility.

- Garlic – an old charm carried, worn and placed around one's home to protect against negative influences.

- Goat – similar to a bull is worn to increase virility and for protection.

- Goldfish – because fish symbolize abundance and prosperity, and goldfish are brown until they mature, which causes them to turn gold. Goldfish are asymbols of prosperity through hardwork. Placed in the home to avert the evil eye directed towards one's finances.

- Head (Man) – charm of a head or even an item with a man's head can be used to represent (in general) a person's head, mind, and even his soul. Worn or carried to symbolize recovery from a headache or migraine. Silver dimes were once worn to protect the soul for this reason. Small photos nowadays are used in the same manner.

- Head (Woman) – same as head for men.

- Heart – used to symbolize devotion and love. Can also be used to protect one's soul, since the heart is the abode of the human soul/consciousness.

- Hens – are associated with Oset (Aset, Auset, Isis in Greek) symbolize the mothering and nurturing concept. It can be used to also represent one's mother. Carried, worn or placed around the home to symbolize care, concern and protection over one's children. Also can be used as a symbol of prosperity representing careful observance over one's eggs (affairs), a pun ensuring that one lays good eggs.

- Horse – symbolizes a journey can be worn for safe travel. Also symbolize power, hence horsepower, thus can be used assist in stamina.

- Horseshoe – has several meanings depending upon the culture. It symbolizes the shoe of a workhorse and a bowl, therefore it is hung with the open ends up. To ensure that one's luck is retained and doesn't escape. When identified with champion, warriors or soldiers and/or spirits like Hruaakhuti, St. George and other strong figures on horseback defeating serpents and dragons. It symbolizes with open end up, power over evil.

- House – used to attract blessings to one's home and all who dwell there. When traveling can symbolize safe return.

- Leg – similar to an arm charm, is used to represent a condition associated with the leg, knee, ankle or foot. It can also be used to symbolize a journey and strength in one's legs.

- Lion – is carried or worn for physical strength, courage and authority.

- Lotus Flower – used to represent blessings.

- Mule – like the horse can be used to symbolize work. Because the mule is similar to a donkey, which is associated with Set. It can be used to remind one not to be a stubborn jackass and overcome their fears and inhibitions.

- Nefer – symbolizes beauty and goodness.

152

- Owl – for some symbolizes death but for others knowledge. Can be carried or worn to attract to good luck.

- Praying Hands – symbolize faith and can be worn to remind one to trust in the unknown.

- Praying Man – can be used to encourage one's father, brother, husband, etc. To be faithful.

- Praying Woman – same as Praying Man.

- Pyramid – reminds us of balance, ingenuity, determination, precision and hard work. They are associated with Osar (Asar, Ausar or Osiris in Greek). Worn or carried improve work habits, help in breaking destructive habits (like addictions), increase concentration. Crystal pyramids are said to enhance one's psychic abilities and promote emotional balance.

- Ram – similar to the bull and goat, can be used to increase male virility and strengthen one's determination and physical prowess.

- Rings – symbolize unity, togetherness and wholeness. They are worn to promote unity between people, unity of mind and body, unity or perfect health and so on.

- Worn as amulets to treat illness, dispel forces of evil, keep lovers together, and prevent flight of the soul from the body.

- Roosters – symbolize pride, determination and victory. Worn, carried or placed around the home for protection from negative forces and to prevent abuse.

- Scarab – symbolizes the beginning and corresponds to the Khepera moment.

- Seven African Power tools – are seven tools symbolizing the seven most popular orishas in Latin America. It can be used to bring about general luck.

- Shark Tooth – shark teeth are worn by surfers in Hawaii and other parts of the world, to protect against shark attacks. They can also be used to protect against gossip and other vicious verbal attacks like baskbiting.

- Skeleton Key- symbolizes doors of opportunity.

- Skull – symbolizes the ancestors and/or spirits and is used to help break addiction.

- Sma – symbolizes the lungs and was once used by the Kamitic people to give breath to the deceased in the other world.

- Stars – symbolize mysteries, ancestors that rest in the belly of Nut in KAMTA, and also unknown benevolent forces. They are used to ward off evil influences and attract good fortune.

- Sun – symbolizes fame, glory, prosperity, success and friendship.

- Tassels – such as the bunch of chords on a graduation cap, is an ancient charm found in Kamit to symbolize happiness. Used to represent the completion of a project. In other areas however, the tassels are believed to deter negative spirits due to the numerous cords.

- Tet – When worn or carried, the tet also known as Oset (Aset or Isis Buckle) promotes good health, fertility and strengthens one's psychic abilities. Since it symbolizes the female genitalia, it also is believed to increase a woman's sex appeal.

- Tiger – is carried or worn for physical strength.

- Tulip Bulb – similar to the Tet due to its shape, a tulip bulb as carried or worn can attracts new love, increases sex appeal and improves fertility.

- Turtle – symbolize longevity, stamina, fertility, intelligence sexuality, physical protection and spiritual protection.

This is just a partial listing, so feel free to explore the common symbols that appear in your life and use them as charms. Remember that what makes a charm powerful is how you use it and the power you imbue into them. Used as a programming language for your sahu, they make a great way to communicate to your aakhu and netcharu, which we explore in the next chapter.

Chapter 7:
Creating a Magical Way of Life

Remember, it is the consequences of our actions that influence the type of assistance we will receive. If you focus on negative thoughts they will yield negative actions and manifest negative entities in our life. These negative energies become the negative and destructive people that surrender to their Set and perform chaotic deeds, which is why the Kamitic thinkers called these energies snakes. Whereas by focusing on positive thoughts, they will yield positive actions, which in turn produce positive spiritual influences in our life. We basically create or better yet, attract our own angels and devils because they are archetypes of our psyche.

As I stated throughout this book, we all have aakhu (ancestors and spirit guides) and netcharu (guardian spirits) because they are energetic principles that influence our life. We have had these principles in our life since the beginning of time and the only reason most of us cannot identify with them as compared to how our ancestors did is because, in these modern times. Due to the separation of church and state, we favor physical sciences over the metaphorical spiritual science. When in actuality we should truly be embracing both. Consequently, we are skeptical about anything we cannot understand using our five physical sciences, which is natural, but sooner or later. We have to realize that there is only so far we can get using our physical senses. This is a point that I was force to come to grips with when I read *Think & Grow Rich*, by Napoleon Hill.

Napoleon Hill, for those who do not know, is considered the pioneer of personal success literature. Many of the techniques he learned and wrote about in his bestselling book, now classic, was tried and true methods from the late 19th and early 20th century millionaires of the time. Most of the methods Hill wrote about were well received but one of the techniques was so controversial that he hesitated on even mentioning. In the end he decided to include it in the book, and it was called the nine Invisible Counselor techniques.

According to Hill, the Invisible Counselors technique was the ultimate tool for sourcing skills, ideas and inspiration. Using this visualization technique Hill claimed that he was able to tap into the mind of anyone living or dead in order to gain advice, wisdom and guidance. Hill admitted to having conversations with Jesus, Abraham Lincoln, Socrates, Aristotle, Plato, Thomas Edison, Homer, Isaac Newton, Burbank and many others.

Hill revealed that the technique he used to talk to his counselors was that just before going to sleep at night. He would close his eyes and visualize his invisible counselors siting around a counsel table. Before meeting with them he had in mind an objective of something he wanted to achieve and he would allow his counselors to speak freely and give suggestions on how to achieve a certain goal. He said while the meeting with his counselors was purely fictional and existed only in his imagination. His counselors began to take on characteristics that they were real. Through his counselors Hill claimed that he was able to resolve a lot of problems, which led him down a glorious path of adventure.

I only included Hill's technique to show by comparison what he was doing, is no different from what traditional spiritual workers have been doing for centuries. The point I want to focus upon is as stated earlier; it is a known fact that many of the early 20th century artists, entrepreneurs, inventors and innovators were aware of the power of the mind. Many of these individuals were known for going to sleep in order to solve a problem or get an idea, which is how shamans help to heal people in their community. There are numerous comments and quotes that have been recorded by many of the early 20th century visionaries like Thomas Edison who said that "Ideas come from space," clearly indicating that many of them didn't know how or why all human beings had the ability to create change in their life by stretching out into the great unknown using their imagination. They just knew that they could do it and they took full advantage of it. I say all of this because we have reached the part of the book that will appear to be more fiction than science. I have tried to where possible to give the scientific reasoning as to why a method works, which is why a great amount of time, was spent talking about KAMTA and TASETT to help prepare you for this

157

point. But now the time has come to go way beneath the horizon and beyond our logical reasoning.

Before we descend down the proverbial rabbit hole, it is important to keep in mind that when your ab – soul awareness is extroverted, attention is placed on physical things outside of your being, because you are identifying with your physical environment through your sahu (subconscious awareness). However, when your ab – soul is introverted, attention is placed on the non-physical reality that exists within of your being, because you are identifying with the spirit that exists in all things through your ba (superconscious), which gives us unlimited ability to gain ideas and information to accomplish anything we set our mind to. Therefore, in order to achieve any objective in life, it has to be firmly impressed upon our sahu that we can achieve it. This is the only way for our ba to make a way for it to manifest physically, which simply means if you want magic or a miracle to occur in your life. You have to believe. It doesn't matter what anyone else believes. It is all about what you believe.

With this in mind you need to remember that ideas about what we can achieve are impressed upon our sahu using our emotions, so the more intense are emotions are associated with an idea, the stronger the impression will be made upon our sahu. This is the reason shocking and also traumatic experiences have a long-term affect upon our psyche. However, ideas can also be impressed upon our sahu through repetition, using symbols, etc. One way of looking at it is that the odder and stranger it appears logically, the stronger the impression it will make upon our psyche.

This is the mindset that you have to adopt and develop in order create a miraculous way of life. It is difficult (but not impossible) for most people in the West because Westerners have a problem seeing that everything is interconnected. This is partially due to the fact that most Westerners see God only as a point of reference for when things go wrong. When in need, we raised in the West are taught to plead to God for help because we are pathetic human beings born in sin. When our prayers aren't answered, we believe that God is punishing us for something we've done. As a result, every tragedy and tragic event is seen as God punishing us for something that we've done. So God from the Western perspective is not truly worshipped out of love, but out of fear. It is because of this fear, many will not even attempt to better their lives by praying for worldly goods and will instead choose to live with illness, in poverty and other unbearable conditions, believing it is God's will.

On the other hands, the inability to see the interconnectedness of things makes others believe that in order to create miracles all they have to do is master a few spells like Harry and his friends of Hogwart; throw together some herbs, stones and some obnoxious smelling substance and "*Voila*" they will get a job, love and everything they want; or just visualize their goals, think positive and they will physically manifests whatever they want into their life, all from the comfort of their home. Then when the spiritual system doesn't work or it doesn't resolve their problems. They say it is fraudulent or that it is superstitious nonsense. Never do these individuals take the time to explore why they failed to achieve their goal through supernatural means, because they don't see how everything is interdependent upon one another.

The fact is that magic and miracles are based upon the invisible, spiritual forces that exist in KAMTA and visible, physical work done in TASETT. It begins in the deep recesses of our mind and finishes with our physical efforts. It is not based upon what you think or theorize, but upon how you feel. This is the reason all people regardless of their affiliations, beliefs, background, etc. are amazed when they see the pyramids, the temples, the sphinx and all of the other mysteries of Kamit. It is because Kamit strikes a serious chord deep within our collective consciousness that transcends all of the superficial things that separate us today. She reminds people of a time when magic and miracles was a common place before dogma dominated the world scene. It is for this reason, I can't fault anyone for wanting to recreate this magical and miraculous time in human history, but reality of this happening is just not feasible because what people faced during those times are not the same type of problems we have today. We can however, use their wisdom to improve the quality of our life by adopting a holistic view of life.

Everything from a non-Western perspective is seen as being interdependent upon something else. God from the non-Western perspective is seen as being the Creator of Everything or Source but also is believed to have given everything that exist a piece of its power in order for it to sustain its existence. So when an individual becomes ill or needs divine assistance from a non-Westerner perspective, they don't view it as it being a curse from God. They understand that the predicament they are in is because of an incorrect choice or decision they have made in God's absence. In other words, non-Westerners take responsibility of their actions and behaviors. Instead of blaming their shortcomings on the devil, they accept that most of their problems are their own doing, due to them not having the exact know-how or not knowing God's will, who has the final say in everything. Because non-Westerners see God and themselves as being interdependent upon each other, in dire circumstances some non-Western cultures when they really need divine assistance will provoke God in order to make the Divine angry. Such as the women in the Kongo when in emergency situations, would expose their breast to God and make him angry, so that he will act[27]. This behavior is shocking to many Westerners because they don't share the same cultural perspective, but when we take into account the ba and sahu relationship. It becomes clear that this shocking action is meant to get the ba to provide a creative and intuitive solution quickly.

Again, failure to understand that our sahu is responsible for all of the life changes that occur in our life is the reason most people are unsuccessful in changing their behavior. It has to be remembered that you can't change an individual's conscious by just reading a scripture or prayer because the idea will not be impressed upon the sahu (subconscious part of our being). A change in conscious and any individual's life can only occur when an individual is truly moved or a deep emotional impression is made upon their sahu, resulting in them changing. So, to help you to create a magical and miraculous way of life, the following abilities needed to be kept in mind. These have been modified from the seven codes listed in Maa.

---

[27] Rockie, Simon. Death and the Invisible Power: The World of Kongo Belief, 1993. pg. 136

The Seven Divine Abilities

The Divine Ability to Disperse

The ability to disperse energy depends upon your ability to remember that God through our ba does not function according to time and space. It is not bound by earthly logic. This means if you want to impress the idea of your body being healed. All you need to do is contemplate on being healthy or in perfect health. Eventually, when the idea become habitual. It will be accepted by the sahu as truth and you will begin to feel and act as if you are healthy. Thereby becoming healthier. All spiritual solutions are based upon the ability to focus on a solution and not the condition itself.

The Divine Ability to Be At Peace

Now, it is very important that you understand, that this also means that you have to be patient. This is because your blessings may not manifest exactly when you want them to. This is the time when a lot of people become discouraged because they were praying for a blessing or miracle in their marriage, on their job, in their family, etc. and it has not occurred yet when they wanted to. At this time, you need to be patient and trust that your Osar knows more than you. Don't force the issue and try to force a solution. Keep the faith and stay focused. When you begin to question things or become discouraged. Sometimes you will receive a message of encouragement from an unlikely source, but keep the faith and stay patient.

The Divine Ability to Direct

Because God's Rau exist everywhere and in everything, a divine mind has the ability to direct this energy at will to achieve a specific goal. This is the difference between a human being and an animal. In order to develop a divine mind, you have to learn how to act with purpose instead of reacting to life. This means always questioning and reviewing the goal, objective and purpose behind whatever you do, to ensure that

161

you are not being ruled by your sahu. Remember, the best way to manifest a goal is to make it so that it benefits others.

The Divine Ability to Manifest

The importance of single-mindedness is only to teach you to live and focus your attention in the now. Far too often, the reason so many people have high blood pressure and other ailments is because they worry about the future. They don't understand that worrying never fixes anything. The best thing to do is to live in the present because it is our present actions that determine our future. This is the beauty of life. Whenever we approach something that we do not like. All we have do to is project what it is that we want in the now, to create the change we want later.

The Divine Ability to Bless

Whenever you acknowledge something that is pleasing, beautifying and enhancing. Whenever you appreciate something and demonstrate an act of kindness. You are in essence blessing it. Blessings exemplify what we want out of life and they help us to receive blessings in return. Take something as simple as opening the door for someone. If you genuinely open the door for someone to help them, you will find that other complete strangers will open the door for you. I remember, I always spoke to people by offering a warm "Hello," to them. Then, one day when I went out of town. I found a lot of strangers willing to greet me. So, a divine mind has the ability to bless others because they understand that they are in essence blessing themselves. They do this physically but telepathically as well.

The Divine Ability to Empower

As I have already mentioned in the start of this book. The Kamitic people were fond of empowering things by personifying them. Anything can be personified because it is all from God's Rau. Just because something does not move does not mean that God's essence is not in it. It simply means that it is vibrating at a very low rate. When you begin to see everything as being a living being, you will see how some places like cemeteries, hospitals, houses, parks, etc. have energies of their own. You will be able to determine the character of certain places and discern the spiritual remedy needed in that area. I have heard of other shamans passing through a park and changing the energy of it by simply blessing stones. Each time that passed by the park they would bless another stone and put it wherever the stone chose to be. Eventually, the park became a haven of good and blessed spirits, which encourage families to visit it.

The Divine Ability to Create

Our sahu tends to make us think that creativity deals with just creating things like artwork, music, poetry, etc. to get money or an exchange of services. This is a low perspective of thinking and there is nothing wrong with it, but I invite you to go beyond this and think of creating as a means of changing lives. When you enter the creation process from the ba perspective, it takes on a whole new meaning. For instance, sex is not just an act performed between a man and woman who are attracted to each other. From a ba perspective, it is the creation of the universe in physical form. The sexual relationship between a male and female is actually the physical mimicking of Divine to create life in the universe.

So, you have to think in a new way when you are developing a divine mindset. Everything that you do is done for a specific purpose. A regular conversation between you and your coworker is about transforming both of your minds so that you both have a productive and successful workday. A conversation between your spouses is about helping each other to reach their potential. Talking to your children is about encouraging them to listen to their ba and so on, because the divine ability to create is the ability to bring godliness in everyone's life. Everything has purpose, even the placement of plants in your house.

163

All of these abilities you will see depend largely upon your intuition, which is a mental faculty of your ba. It is not hard, it only seems this way because you are not use to following your ba, but with practice it will become easier and easier. All of these keys will come into play when we explore working with the netcharu are divine helpers.

The Gods Were People Too!

Hill's discovery made me realize that because God is all knowing, all-powerful and like any good parent, could give us whatever we need to succeed in life, except live our life for us. This means that whatever I wanted to know and needed, there was an answer or remedy. That remedy could be looked upon as a spiritual medicine, which archeologists and historians called gods and goddesses. But this is incorrect, because this assumes that ancient people were primitive and just made up gods and goddesses to suit their liking. This made me wonder if the Kamitic people created their so-called gods and goddess like Hill had created his invisible counselors.

So I decided to research the subject and what I discovered was that when the Hyskos, a mixed race of people from the West of Asia, invaded Lower Kamit, and ruled the region for a number of years until they were expelled, were followers of Set. The fact that these invaders and the Kamitic people knew about Set meant that Set initially was a human being who was immortalized as a mythical character in the human psyche. There is historical evidence that also reveals that Osar was most likely modeled after the legendary king Menes (also known as Narmer), who was the first to unite the kingdom. His successor was the first dynastic king named Hr-Aha or Hru Aha, hence the mythical Hru.

So, if the so-called gods and goddesses were once people. It would mean that they were immortalized or forever remembered for what they had done. This is why after understanding who and what Set is, it is incorrect to call the netcharu gods and goddesses because that is like saying that Set is a god, which is like saying the Devil or Satan is a god too, which we know is not the case. We do know that Set is a strong and immortal force, which explains the reason why the Kamitic

164

philosophers called these invisible beings netcharu (also spelled neters or neteru, also called angels).[28]

Accepting the netcharu (the so-called gods and goddesses of Kamit) were once people, explains the reason behind the various Kamitic practices. It means that just like Hill was able to tap into the mind of the living and dead. The Kamitic shamans discovered this technique thousands of years before he had and the person that taught him. This made it possible for all of the Kamitic people to have a:

- Luck counselor that helps us find better opportunities to improve our lot in life.
- Success counselor that helps us to achieve our goals.
- Health counselor that gives us advice regarding our health.
- Financial wealth counselor that helps us with our finances and teaches us everything about the power of money.
- Relationship counselor that helps us to understand love, working with others and the safe way to have fun and enjoy life.
- Security and defense counselor that teaches us how to protect ourselves from external dangers, and much, much more.

But unlike Hill that chose to meet with his invisible counselors only when he retired to bed. The Kamitic people (like other shamanic cultures) interacted with these counselors, their spiritual clan leaders by creating icons and using these symbols to represent the netchar. But they were talked to just the same. Like Hill, noticed the peculiarities of his counselors, it was discovered that the netcharu were uncomfortable in a certain places, things and events that occurred in history. In other words, Osar for instance, does not like alcoholic beverages because the historic Osar was probably poisoned using alcohol. No one knows because his factual-story has been lost in the sands of times, since it occurred in pre-dynastic times, but the truth of his story has been commemorated, memorized and now serves as a model.

---

[28] The term is spelled with 'tch' because the etymology of the word suggests that it should be pronounced with a "ch" and not with a "t" sound as in the word "nature," which coincidentally is derived from the Kamitic word Neter or Netchar.

It was this understanding that taught me a lot about the netcharu and most importantly a lot about myself, which is why one of the most important lessons you need to master is how to distinguish between your own wayward thoughts and suggestions from other forces. This was the purpose of Exercise 4 and the point of informing you "that you will not be given a vision without provisions." So don't quit your job because you got the hunch to do so, without having another job or some other means of taking care of your financial responsibilities, by claiming that it was divine inspiration. No, that was all you. The netcharu will not lead you astray or inspire you to hurt yourself and others. You will know when they are speaking because you will get a hunch. For instance, you will know when they need light because you may see a candle. You will know when they need cigar smoke, because a pack of cigars might fall in front of you. You will know they have heard your petition because during conversation with someone, a solution suddenly appears. It is little synchronicities that will help you to learn more about these essences. You just have to trust your intuition.

Now, similar to how Hill began with his counselors, in order to work with the netcharu you have to establish a rapport with them. As I have stated in the previous two chapters, I suggest that you do not begin communicating with your netcharu until your aakhu have chosen to introduce you to them. Only after you feel drawn to the netcharu should you try to establish a rapport with them. You will know when they are calling to you or that your aakhu (ancestors) are introducing you to them because all of a sudden. You may find a particular object that you have passed by on the street for some odd reason appealing to you. You could have a dream and in the dream it is revealed to you that you should have something like a seashell, which you find very easy to obtain. Until that time comes I suggest that you read over the material and familiarize yourself with how the netcharu manifest themselves in our life. This way when they do make their presence known and you are introduced to them by your aakhu. You will be prepared for them to take a more active role in your life.

Everyone has different approaches or ways as to how they deal with these archetypical spirits. Contrary to what some may believe,

166

there is no right or wrong way. The only right way is what works for you based upon your understanding, spiritual maturity and gets you tangible results. The wrong way, is of course the opposite. Your relationship between you and your netcharu, similar to your aakhu, is based upon a *quid pro quo* system, which is Latin meaning, "you give me something I give you something in return." So the same way you wouldn't expect a complete stranger to come up to you and give you a million dollars. You shouldn't expect God and your guardians to bless you with a million dollars if you don't have a relationship with the Divine. Yes, God is by theory all-knowing but from a practical perspective just because God knows you need help. God is not going to help you because God doesn't know you. God from a non-Western perspective would treat you like an applicant for a bank loan. God would have to check your credentials, and this is why so many people believe that their prayers go unanswered because they only come to God when in dire need.

When it comes to working with these archetypes this same sort of relationship exists in non-Western traditions. Although our spirits have been around and watching over us since birth, they are strangers to us and we to them, because we have not had a formal introduction and do not have a rapport with one another. The rapport is built through a partnership, which means that at any time you feel like you giving more then you should. You can end the partnership. In fact, if you feel like your netcharu are making some pretty unusual requests that you can't fulfill. You can end the partnership. Your partnership with your netcharu (and for that matter you aakhu) should be beneficial to both parties (you and them). If it isn't then end it. At the same time, don't expect your aakhu and netcharu to be doing things without proper payment either. If they feel like they are being taken advantage of or misused in any way, they will end the partnership as well.

Now, here's one of the beauties of working with your aakhu and netcharu. It is that because you are focused on tangible results, no one has to beg you to do anything. This is not a religion but a way of life. This is not like being forced to attend religious service out of obligation. No. You do this because you see the tangible benefit of doing so as if you were going to a job to get a paycheck. It is that simple. If you don't

167

see any benefit, you do not have to work with the netchar. You can simply stop and move on.

Working the Kamitic Faith

As I mentioned before, I credit my success in establishing a rapport with my netcharu and working with them to Papa, because of the unique way he described how to work with them. Papa who believed his orishas (guardian spirits) were all warriors, sat close to the ground, as warriors often do in order to be alert and aware of their environment. Papa told me that the only reason people began creating altars and placing their spirits on high pedestals was because this was how Europeans viewed God. This was not the case in Africa where the divinities were seen as being human beings that were deified in death. So, whenever I went to Papa's house and he did any spiritual work. We sat on the floor right alongside his orishas.

One day I remembered, I asked who was his warriors fighting he told me it was the devil. In fact, he told me that when there was a thunderstorm it was the orisha of thunder and lightning, Chango, and the orisha of war, Oggun, fighting the devil. It took a while for me to truly understand what he meant by this story, which he had creolized but I finally got it. As a result, I followed suit and unlike most African traditional systems that didn't believe in the existence of a devil or the epitome of evil. I accepted that the devil existed based upon the Kamitic spiritual systems and acknowledged that his name was Set. But, Set was not like the devil in Christian lore that wages war against his Creator God for control of the throne. In the Kamitic spiritual tradition, Set is the symbol of everything we do not want to be. He is the archetype of man and woman at their lowest, controlled by their weaknesses and prone to resolving problems through violence.

So, I began establishing a rapport with my netcharu similar to the way Papa did but with my own personal flare. I identified with my netcharu as being warriors. By following Papa's advice and examples, I discovered that my netcharu were warriors and united to fight against Set. It was from this metaphorical observation that I learned that none of the netcharu space should ascend above eye level. Only God was above eye level, which is why the Eye of Ra was used to symbolize Amun Ra and is placed above the altar.

It was by using similar visual techniques that I saw Set as the epitome of evil and the netcharu as my own personal clan of protectors against his catastrophes. The netcharu appeared to be individuals with special talents devoted to a common cause from this perspective. However after much trial and error, I noticed that in order to succeed in creating a miraculous way of life by working with them. There were certain things I had to do in regards to my own development. I realized that my success with the netcharu depended upon my relationship with my aakhu. It was this personal experience that made me realize that fiction and non-fiction writers, filmmakers, and many others, have seriously warped our perception of who and what the netcharu are. Most of the descriptions about the Kamitic spiritual practices have been excessively romanticized because many Westerners have a fear of death. This is why I find it very odd that although a number of writers claim that the Kamitic people believed in this and that based upon a wall painting, a sacred texts that was recovered (such as the *Pert em Hru*, the so-called *Book of the Dead*), etc. None of these writers ever speak about how most of the grand edifices of Kamit were shrines and tombs to deceased leaders. These same writers never mention anything about the sacred objects found in the tombs with the mummified rulers, such as the host of charms and ushabti dolls with small holes in their back, which are very similar to the type of dolls that have been found in various parts of Africa, the Caribbean, Brazil and the American South.

The Kamitic people did not have an obsession with death nor did they worship death. They understood a basic truth, which was that regardless of who you are and what you have or have not accomplished. We will eventually die because death does not discriminate between young and old, rich and poor. No one can cheat or outwit death and in this regards. The Kamitic people did not fear death. What they feared was like most people today, how they died and how they would be remembered. It was from their ancestors they learned that if one lived in the most horrible manner like Set. Generally speaking they died in a horrible manner and were vaguely remembered. If however one lived in an ethical manner like Osar, they were missed when they passed into the spirit realm and honored for eternity.

The truth about the Kamitic faith can be found in the tombs of the Kamitic rulers in plain sight. The reasons most have refused to acknowledge it is because they are in denial that the Kamitic faith was based upon the relationship between the living (Hru) and the honorable dead (Osar). The theory behind working with one's ancestors is that the only way to figure out what you need to do in order to get to heaven. You need to talk to someone who is already in heaven, which are your enlightened and honorable ancestors. Everything that was mentioned throughout this book about self-control, self-development, and self-mastery was because the aakhu discovered that in the spiritual realm, the spirits that were the most evolved were the ones that were closer to the Divine Source or God. It was the ancestors that helped humanity understand the greatest mystery of all, which is what happens after death. And, this is the reason ancestor veneration is the most widely practiced tradition around the world.

Working with the netcharu basically consisted of conducting various rituals and observing specific taboos as it related to the netcharu. This was necessary as anyone familiar with the shamanic practice of journeying, the *Pert em Hru* or the *Bardo Thodol* (the so-called Tibetan Book of the Dead) will understand because it leads to deeper levels within the human psyche, described as various levels, doors, halls, etc. that were described in these ancient texts.

In Kamit (and other African societies that were influenced by Kamit such as the Kongo people), this metaphoric relationship gave rise to a whole host of ritual complexities and the observance of specific taboos based upon ancestor's specifications. In other words, as I have said before, nothing in shamanic culture is done without purpose. As a result, the reason for honoring and venerating the honorable dead was to learn from them and their experience. The netcharu are the ones that allow us to interact with our ancestors safely.

Paying Spiritually For What You Want

Remember, even though we human beings love to categorize things and try to make sense of the things in Nature. Nature does not always conform to the order we place it in. Nature is very magical and depends upon energy. Energy works on exchange, meaning what you put in is what you get back in return and vice versa. It is what is called in Latin *quid pro quo* that translates to "I give you something, you give me something." This basically means you don't get something for nothing. To understand how this concept works with the netcharu, if a stranger walked up to you and asked for $50 would you give it to them? Most likely not and the reason is because you don't know that individual. Right? Well, if it were a family member or a best friend that asked for that money. You would feel more inclined to give them the $50 because you would have a greater chance of getting the money back in return. The reason is because you know them. You know where they live, where they work and when they get paid. Even if a little doubt crosses your mind about getting the money back. For the most part you expect to have the money returned to you. If you didn't get the money back you know that you would get something back as repayment from them because you have a rapport with this individual. The same occurs when you make offerings to your spiritual allies. You are in essence building a relationship between them and you.

One of the ways to do this is by making your request and listening to their response. Once you receive a response from them, just like you express your gratitude from a gift receive from someone unexpectedly. You offer a word of thanks for their assistance. If you give them an offering of one of their favorite things such as flowers in their color, food and even money, they will be more inclined to help you knowing that you will give them something in return.

For instance, whenever I am in a bind and need Npu to help me with a solution. Sometimes, it requires that I offer him a pipe cigar, some candy and rum to help me clean up a problem. But, I have found that if I had enlisted his help in the beginning, it doesn't cost as much. It is sort of like preventive medicine. So, whenever I have to drive anywhere I always offer him a little gift so that I have safe trip to and

171

from my destination. I would prefer to do this versus wishing I had done it after some unfortunate event. Remember, this is all about energy.

Another popular offering is to give to a charity, either monetarily or through volunteer work, but a lot of time we try to avoid this type of spiritual work because we don't want to be taken advantage of. I remember when I use to live in Detroit I would give the man who came to clean the windows of my car a dollar, until I learned that my best friend's uncle who was a professional con man claimed to know some of these people. After learning that, whenever I saw people begging for money I always thought that they could be scam artists, so I would pass them by. It wasn't until I experienced hardship myself and learned about the Yoruba Sokar, Babaluiye that I began to think that maybe these individuals could have a serious need. I wondered how do, you know if your offering of charity is really being used for good or if you are being scammed. Then my Osar informed me that the only way is to trust my intuition. Charity is not supposed to be given in the first place for recognition. It is given to assist others in a time of need. I was showed that if I genuinely give from my heart, not to worry about if the individual is genuine or fraudulent, because the reason I was giving in the first place was to help myself, since we are all connected. Now, I let the spirit determine who is fraudulent and who is not. I was, reminded by this situation that, I need to continue to follow my spirit. The reason is because again our universe functions, on the *quid pro quo* system. By me being charitable, one day another will be charitable to me. It is an example of a ritualistic gesture.

Now, a lot of people influenced by Westernize religions will scoff at the idea of making offerings as being primitive, so let me explain the theory behind this and clarify it for you. Many times when we receive a blessing or gift, there is a part of us (our ego) that makes us feels that we don't deserve the gift if it is free. It this same part of us that rejects pity and suspects that when a gift is given for free that something must be wrong with it. So offerings also make us feel a sense of self-worth. They make us appreciate what we are receiving. At times it will feel like we are bribing the spirits and when you feel this way. It is the natural guilt coming from your ego. To remove this feeling you simply need to give more.

172

I guarantee you that the more you give the less guilty you will feel. In fact, one of the best offerings to give to your spirits is money, which is somewhat equivalent of animal sacrifices in many traditional societies. The way to give money is to write out your request on a brown piece of paper such as a piece of brown paper bag. Then take the request and burn it. Next, take a dollar bill and hold it between your hands. Then talk to the netcharu or aakhu, while rubbing the money between your hands. Next, place it in their lap imbued with your request. You can do this with any dollar amount. I would however recommend that when giving money that you use dollar bills only because to some spirits. If you offer a number of them, it will appear to be a lot of money.

It is through this ritual gesture you will find another myth somewhat debunked which is that you can't take money with you into the spiritual realm. No, not physically, but you can take currency into the spiritual realm because there is a sort of currency that exists there. In fact you will find that the netcharu and aakhu like money a lot. This is a fact that many Asian businesses have known for years, which is why despite Communist reform the Chinese practice of giving money and burning hell money is still practiced. Now, what do the netcharu and aakhu do with the money is not known. What is known is that occasionally they will intuitively ask you to take the money you have offered, to purchase something that they like or give it to someone in need.

It is important that when you are making offerings to the netcharu and aakhu that you tell them what it is that you want. Never leave it in their hands as to what you want. I wouldn't leave my fate in their hands because the lack of a physical body prevents them from physically measuring and accessing what should be done. It is best to tell them what you want and let them find the easiest way available to help you make what you want a physical reality.

It is in this exchange that all thoughts that the netcharu and aakhu are worshipped will be laid to rest because when you began paying them for what you want. You will see very quickly once you begin the above practice that these are truly allies on the other side of our universe. As you continue to make these offerings you will slowly find that it increases your faith, thereby empowering your rapport with your ba/Osar.

Welcoming Your Spiritual Guardians

According to Kamitic theory we each have nine major netcharu (including Osar) that accompany us from the moment of birth. Since, Kamitic spirituality is the oldest tradition in the world and the predecessor of African spirituality, I tend to think of the netcharu as being ancient clan leaders or tribal heads. The netcharu established a spiritual clan so that when they are called upon unexpectedly and they are not present. A spiritual helper that is akin to the netchar can address the request that was put forth. Consequently, most of the netcharu are placed on the second tier of the altar, while some like Npu, Hruaakhuti and Maat, prefer to walk or stand, alone. Just like the first tier, a cross or some icon referring to the awesomeness of God needs to be placed on the altar. I suggest placing either a cross or the Eye of Ra above the altar. This again is a reminder that the no petition can be granted without the Divine's say so.

Now, the analogy of the second tier altar is simple, since the netcharu are of a higher vibration they are slightly above our aakhu. Their influence therefore pass descends to our aakhu, which is then transferred to us. From a psychological perspective it can be said that the netcharu acts as archetypes residing in the collective unconscious. Our aakhu, the surviving ascendants in the spiritual realm turn to the netcharu when we want something and give us the instructions we need in the form of an inspirational idea. This idea manifests itself physically when choose to consciously act upon it.

So, the netcharu exist in our psyche whether we believe in them or not. They are personified in order to help us better understand our selves and the universe around us. The netcharu are not worshipped because they are not God. They are thought to be superhuman beings that are communicated with as one would work with a friend. The best way I found to learn about them is relating to using historical and fictional characters, which we see in movies.

Osar: The Lord of KAMTA

Purpose: Justice and Wisdom
Colors: All White, White and Silver, White and Blue
Sacred Number: All numbers
Places in Nature: Underground and Mountains
Sacred Space: Place on the het (unless otherwise specified)

Although we have talked about Osar in great detail, think of your Osar as a great patriarch in your kingdom. The Lord of the Underworld – KAMTA –is the netchar over wisdom, knowledge and peace. He helps you to resolve issues peacefully and shows you how you can achieve your objectives the least amount of problems. He is wise, full of good counsel and he has a powerful influence. He is someone you can turn as a last result, like the fictional character Don Corleone played Marlon Brando in *The Godfather*[29]. Osar's colors are white and he is fond of all things white. Osar, however does not accept any alcoholic beverages since it was used by Set to overthrow him.

His favorite symbol is the djed column also called Osar's backbone, symbolizing strength. Your Osar will be fond of all things white because they symbolize coolness, purity, knowledge, patience and wisdom.

Npu: Opener of the Way

Purpose: For Luck
Colors: Black and Red or Black, Red and White
Sacred Number: 3 and 21
Day of the Week: Wednesday
Sacred Space: Place on the floor near the front door (unless otherwise specified)

---

[29] Unfortunately, there are not a lot of films that depict fathers in a strong light. Most films either portray fathers as being comical, stubborn patriarchs like the comedian Steve Martin in Father of the Bride and Cheaper by the Dozen, or as evil and horrible step parents.

If you will recall, when Oset began searching for the body of Osar, she could not find him and didn't get any assistance, until Ra sent forth Npu (Anubis) to assist the desperate queen. This is why everything begins and ends with Npu who is also called Ap-Uat – The Opener of the Way.

Npu is the masked jackal headed man of Kamit. In Brazil he is known as Exu, in Cuba and Trinidad he is called Ellegua and in Haiti, they know him as Papa Legba. Npu is the son of Osar and Nebhet, which explains the reason why he has the spirit of a child and the wisdom of an old man. Because Npu is commonly depicted in murals embodying the dead and is the son of Osar, he is the guardian of the "unnamed and forgotten dead," which is part of the reason he is often confused with the devil. This however is not true. Someone has to guide the lost souls and Npu is the one that has taken on the job. In fact, many believe that when people talking about seeing a light when they die. It is actually Npu returning to take the recently deceased to the other side. As a guide, some associate Npu with the star that guided the wise men to the infant Jesus.

Npu is your personal messenger that delivers messages to other kingdoms (allies and foes alike). He knows everything that is going on because he is trusted with your most valuable secrets. If you imagine Npu as being an employee in your company he is doorman that sees everyone who comes in and leaves. Again, like a perfect doorman he knows everything that is going on like the doorman Ralph Hart in the mid-1970s television series *The Jeffersons*, because he is trusted with valuable information. His loyalty as you can imagine is based upon how well he is treated. Treat him exceptionally well and he will connect you with the right people, at the right time and place. Disrespect him and he will lead you to your doom and even betray you.

His favorite colors are black, red and white. The colors black and red symbolize his ability to move between both realms, while the color white shows his allegiance to Osar. The sacred numbers are 3 and 21. He is associated with the planet Mercury and his sacred days are Wednesday and Monday, since it marks the beginning of the week. Npu is fond of all types of candy, especially candy that is red, sweet and

176

spicy. He enjoys popcorn, peanuts, peanut butter, rum and pipe tobacco and cigars.

Like a master of ceremony, he is linguist and introduces you to all of the other netcharu. For this reason, he is commonly found standing behind front doors of homes and businesses.

Npu the Opener of the Way and Master of the Roads can help you find anything that is lost. He also opens the way when there are obstacles in your path, in order to help you accomplish your dreams. Associated with Joseph the Dreamer, El Nino de Atocha and many more, Npu is fond of candy, peanuts, cigars, rum, coffee, popcorn and toys. Because he can easily be distracted he is given things that will keep him entertained and focused on you. If you treat your Npu right, he will never leave you and be like a loyal friend, but if you abuse and misuse him, in a time of need, he will abandon you. So, it is always a good idea every week to thank him for opening the way for you to be successful and guiding you to your objectives safely, like a good hunting dog. Next tell him to continue to open the way for your success and luck, and to close the doors to those who will do you and those whom you love harm.

He can be called upon for luck in passing exams, improving the mind, concentration, mental power, learning ability, speech, writing, publishing, media concerns, gossip, slander, interviews, brothers, sisters, neighbors, rumors, theft, all areas of study and communication, also astral projection, overcoming addictions, breaking habits.

Oset: Queen Mother of Life

Working with Oset: Queen of the Waters
Purpose: Sustenance
Colors: Blue and White
Sacred Number: 7
Day of the Week: Monday
Sacred Space: Place on the het (unless otherwise specified)

Oset is the wife of Osar and mother of Hru that ensures that you have what you need to live. The mother to us all also shows us how to nurture one another, care for children and the ones we love. She rules over domestic matters, fertility and home surroundings because she is associated with the moon, which governs all issues relating to water. She is also seen as the mother of revolutionary change.

Oset can be thought of as the matriarch of your kingdom that is solely concerned with the wellbeing of everyone within, whom she sees as her own children and family. Oset is suspicious of everyone and questions everyone intention as it relates to her people, because she doesn't want the ones she love to get hurt. So, before she accepts any newcomer into the family, kingdom, organization, etc. They have to prove their loyalty to the group. Because of Oset's psychic motherly instincts, she is able to pick up on an individual's psychic impressions. Her gifts and love for her family, people, etc. allow her at times to act as a spiritual adviser like the fictional character Senora Evalina Montoya played by Celia Cruz in the 1992 film *Mambo Kings* and the fictional character Mo'at played by C.C. H. Ponder, in the film 2009 film *Avatar*. First impressions mean a lot, but Oset is able to see beyond the façade by getting you to pay attention not what a person says but their actions and behavior. But when Set imprisons Oset, it can be easily seen as stirring the winds on the ocean, resulting in a hurricane. Oset could become the evil stepmother or matriarch of legendary lore.

Her colors are is blue like the ocean and white. She is fond of melons, pineapples, grapefruits and other fruits with a lot of seeds. Her totem animals are fish, sheep, seagulls and whales. Sailboats are used to remind us of her legendary voyage to find Osar. Her special day is Monday. Her favorite incense and oils are jasmine, poppy, myrtle, camphor, sandalwood, and opium, which are all hypnotic and meditative.

Hru: The True Heir of the Throne

Purpose: Success, fame, confidence, vitality, increased health, vitality, charisma and protection.
Colors: Red and White, Red and Gold

Day of the Week: Sunday
Sacred Number: 6
Sacred Space: Place on the het (unless otherwise specified)

Hru is a composite of principles because he is our ab soul personified. By composite of principles I mean that he is the heir of Osar, child of Oset, younger brother to Npu, nephew of Hruaakhuti, Nebhet and Set, student of Djahuti, who has been touched (blessed) by Ra. It is for this reason Hru like his uncle Hruaakhuti is full of fire, courage and vitality. He is very manly but handsome. His words can be as sharp as a sword but in the same breath as sublime and sensual because he has a golden tongue. He is the hero of the Kamitic pantheon because his main focus is justice and success, which makes him a powerful strategist.

Hru is not just concerned with defeating his uncle Set. He wants his kingdom and everything that comes with it back in the palm of his hands. He wants all who had anything to do with Osar's death killed and Set brought to his knees. This is Set's influence upon Hru, which has a tendency to make him become consumed by vengeance. When this happens, he is very selfish and will do anything in his power to get what he want even if it means putting innocents in harm's way

But when Hru is guided by Osar, he is courageous, honest and wields power with utmost authority. Men follow him because he fights for them and those who cannot fight because he is the people's champion like the Scottish warrior William Wallace or the fictional character Aragon in *The Lord of the Rings* trilogy.

Classic Hrus always seem to learn by consequences and from the mistakes of others, which is always on their mind every time they do something. This is what makes them such great leaders and distinguishes them from Set, who rules like a tyrant. They identify with the people and do what is best for the people even if it means sacrificing themselves. The classic legend of the Yoruba king Shango illustrates this point, which after abusing his authority, which led to a civil war; it is said in some version. He Hung himself in order to restore balance and bring his people back together.

I remember the first time I heard this legend, I must admit I didn't understand it at all because in many Western stories the hero always live. It was after I saw in the 1984 Brazilian film *Quilombo* by Carlos Dieques, Ganga Zumba the king of the legendary Palmares (the maroon community in Brazil) who made a grave error in trusting Portuguese colonists, resulting in his community's divide. To prevent a civil war from erupting, sacrificed his life to bring his people together to fight for a common cause.

Hru's are not known for doing what is popular at the time but what is right and necessary. Most Hru's always seem to have father issues, like either they loss their father due to a premature death or didn't know their father. Whatever the case, they always seem to learn about manhood (or how to be a hero) from another strong masculine figure that teaches them to be cautious by observing and studying the actions and behaviors of others. In fact, like their uncle Hruaakhuti, Hru's are known to walk a lonely path until they are called to fulfill their purpose or the movement they are inspiring finally gains ground. Until this time happens, like the child Hru who grew up fatherless in the marshes (and in the other urban areas controlled by Set), they usually spend their time honing skills and learning subjects that most warriors would not even consider like foreign language, music, philosophy, esoteric sciences, etc. For instance, you would rarely find Sun Tzu's *Art of War* in Hruaakhuti's library because for one, Hruaakhuti wouldn't even have a library, but you would find it in Hru's.

Hru is associated with fire and thunder during a storm. He shows us how to defeat our enemy. He also shows us how to be honorable, victorious and a true courageous hero in every fight. Hru can help you with fame, charisma, confidence, courage and securing popularity, assistance from those in high places, success, increasing vitality, spiritual prowess and even riches. Hru's colors are red and white. His totem animals are bulls, bull elephants, male lions, rams, white stallions, hawks and falcons. Thunder is his calling card. He is fond of red apples, bananas, okra, stouts, ales and occasionally cigars in some practices. His element is fire and his celestial influence is the Sun.

A Hru influenced by Set, symbolized as in the legend as Set gouging out the eye of Hru, would be like the young, irrational, immature, rash, hotheaded mindless fictional character Caesar played by Armand Assante in *Mambo Kings.* Another rash Hru would be like Santino "Sonny" Corleone, in *The Godfather* series played by James Caan. Whereas a strong Hru for instance, is a strong will, cool and collective individual like the fictional character Michael Corleone played by Al Pacino.

Thank Hru for giving you victory and success. When you need help in overcoming a tough situation or you want to help someone who is struggling. Set a red light on a penny to Hru asking him to bless you or the person you're trying to assist in overcoming the difficulty. Offer Hru beer, strong ales, red beans and white rice. He is fond of red apples, corn, yams, chili peppers and red wine. Because of Osar's death, Hru knows the danger of overconsumption, which is why you will rarely find a mature Hru drunk and addicted to anything pleasurable. Mature Hru's are always aware of their surroundings, alert and conscientious of others. When they do relax and try to enjoy the pleasures of life. They go all out as if they may never have a chance to celebrate life again. Hru therefore enjoys receiving gifts once a challenge has been overcome such as victory in a lawsuit, victory over a competitor, etc., but if the issue is an ongoing battle. The victory will be short-lived, it is only when the war has been completely won that Hru will finally relax and when this happens, and occasionally he accepts a cigar.

Djahuti: The Problem Solver

Purpose: Advise and Help to Overcome Adversity
Colors: Royal Blue and White
Sacred Number: 8
Sacred Space: Place on the het (unless otherwise specified)

Djahuti is the vizier of Osar. His whole purpose is to help you to overcome any adversity. This does not mean that you will not have any problems because as long as you live. You will always have problems. Problems are a part of life because TASETT is a transitional realm that

181

is always undergoing change. Nothing is permanent in TASETT. As the scripture states, "For what is seen is temporary,[30]" but what Djahuti helps us to understand is that nothing is new under the sun, which means that everything that has happened and will happen, has happened once before. This is because the duality of life causes everything to occur in cycle. As a result, everything that rises will fall and vice versa, because the Circle of Life is based upon biological, physiological and spiritual cycles.

There are not many positive examples of how Djahuti appears because most believe that he is a silly, out of touch, mystical hermit sitting in some remote area meditating on the mysteries of the universe. And offering uncanny riddles like Yoda in *Star Wars* that will lead to one's enlightenment, an out–of– his mind egocentric "wise" man like the character Roy Neary played by Richard Dreyfuss in *Close Encounter of the Third Kind* or a corrupt type of patrician that advises the ruler in exchange for monetary gain or sexual favors. All of these models are incorrect because as the *Story of Osar* indicates, Djahuti in all honesty cannot be corrupted because even he knows Set's weaknesses. The reason it is important to address this is because remember our sahu already is anti-spiritual. It fights us on trying to do anything spiritual, so these models must be rejected or else it will discourage us from meeting our Djahuti.

I have tried my best to find a proper model and the only one that comes close even though he is involved in criminal activity is the fictional character Tom Hagen, the lawyer or consigliore (legal advisor/counselor) played by Robert Duval in *The Godfather* series. Disclaimer: I am not in any shape, fashion or form advocating or condoling criminal activity. The point that I am making when we put aside the criminal aspect is that Tom Hagan was the glue that kept the family together by offering sound advice, especially when tempers were high. This is the same thing that Djahuti did after Set usurped the throne by assisting Oset in conceiving, performing rites for Osar, protecting Hru as a child, repairing Hru's damaged eye, replacing

---

[30] "…we look not at the things which are seen, but at the things which are not seen: for the things which are seen *are* temporal; but the things which are not seen *are* eternal." 2 Corinthians 4:18

Oset's diadem, and standing before the tribunal and advocating in Hru's defense. Besides Oset, no one was more loyal and committed to Osar's cause than Djahuti.

Unlike the mystic that is more concerned with understanding the mysteries of the universe to satisfy his or her own curiosity. Djahuti is more concerned with advocating social change, which is why he helped Oset and Hru. If he were just a mystic he wouldn't have done neither because this is not a mystic's aim.

In fact, Djahuti reveals the role that most sages in traditional African spiritual systems fulfilled. The idea of a mystic, off meditating in search of spiritual enlightenment typically didn't and doesn't exist in most traditional African systems. This is a concept derived from Eastern spiritual traditions. This is not to say that there is something wrong with Eastern practices. It is just that it is not traditional African and this is the reason most people have a misconception about who Djahuti is. The true role of Djahuti is to advocate and advise. His He is the patron of diviners, scribes, priests, priestesses and shamans. He is fond of similar gifts that are given to Osar including white wine, gin, light rum, and water.

Nebhet: The Lady of the House

Purpose: All matters of the heart, love, fidelity, harmony, friendship, attraction, reconciliation, attracting money, increase earnings, social functions, pleasure and reconciliation.
Colors: Yellow, Gold, Yellow and Green
Day of the Week: Friday
Sacred Number: 5
Sacred Space: Place on the het (unless otherwise specified)

Nebhet is known as the Lady of the House. She will show you how to find love, joy and happiness the right way. Her colors are yellow, yellow and green and sometimes pink. She is fond of passion fruits, oranges, mangoes, kiwis, strawberries, chocolate, wines, alcoholic coolers, champagne, pumpkins, spinach, honey and all things yellow including spinach and shrimp omelets. Her totem animals are cats of

183

all kinds. Ducks especially toy ducks remind us of how she accompanied Oset to find the missing parts of Osar. She is also fond of peacock feathers and yellow flowers. Thank Nebhet for bringing you peace, love and harmony into your life and home.

Nebhet can be thought of as your personal public relations manager. She is the one that eases things out for you and makes your relationships with others more sociable. That being said, Nebhet loves to look good, she is very flirtatious and she loves to have a good time, but as you can imagine. Her virtue can also be her vice, which Set will easily use to make one addicted to pleasure. At the same time if she is restricted from expressing herself or experiencing any pleasure

One day my wife and I had a real heated discussion because I had worked all day and she was home but didn't cook or anything. I was really upset because whenever I am off. I always cook for her and have dinner waiting for her whenever she gets home. So, I was really upset and I didn't feel like talking to her at all about anything, because this wasn't the first, second or third time, she had done this. It had been going on for a while now and I just never mentioned it. It just all came out that day and I didn't even want to talk to her. Apparently, she felt the same way and she didn't talk to me either. I knew it wasn't healthy for our relationship for us to be angry like we were, so I asked Nebhet for her help and asked her to bring harmony between the both of us. I lit a yellow candle and rubbed a dollar between my hands for her, while making my request. Then I placed the money in her lap and didn't think about the issue anymore. This didn't change the fact that I was still upset with my wife for what she had done.

Anyway, I can't remember how many days it took, but all of a sudden my wife was cordial and loving like she was before. When I came home from work, she had already cooked dinner for me. I cautiously spoke to her and thanked her for cooking, but I thought in the back of my mind, "It will all change the next day. She'll be right back to doing the same thing."

Well, when the next day came, because she got home before I did. She called and asked what I wanted for dinner. Again, she picked dinner up and had it prepared for when I got home, but I still thought that it was a trick and that she was going to stop any day. So, I was stayed angry at her. For the next few days, this routine continued and I stayed angry with her. Then I had a dream.

In the dream, there was a beautiful brown skinned woman in a yellow dress walking towards me. She was gorgeous and when she got close to me. Then I spit in her face. Immediately afterwards I woke up because I knew the lady was Nebhet, but I couldn't believe what I did. As I sat up in the night, wondering why I would have spit in Nebhet's face. It came to me in a loud inner voice. "Why would you ask me for help and then when I show up you reject me?"

I knew then, Nebhet was talking about my wife. I apologized to Nebhet and returned to bed. The next day, I ceased being angry at my upset.

Because Nebhet according to some sources is believed to be married to Set and was a very festive spirit, it is assumed that after she left Set and became forever known as the sister that saved Osar, she then became Ht-hru (Het-Heru or Hathor in Greek), based upon the fact that she was often depicted protecting Osar with her wings (hence, magical amulets) and assisted Oset in childbirth, who later became his wife. Please understand that this is about principles not incestuous physical relationships.

Hruaakhuti: Guardian of Iron

Purpose: Removing obstacles, dealing with enemies, self- confidence, strength, athleticism, competition, justice
Colors: Dark Red or Red and Purple
Sacred Number: 11 sometimes 3 and 7
Day of the Week: Tuesday
Sacred Space: Place on the floor near front door, next to Npu

In United States there is an idiom we use called "the last straw," which is based upon the old saying, "the straw that broke the camel's back." It is a reference to the fact that camels can carry large loads, but they can still be overburdened. So the idiom "the last straw" means that, that was your last chance, you have reached the limit and are truly gotten on an individual's nerves. I tend to think of Hruaakhuti as such because when you finally meet him. You are about to experience the pain.

Hruaakhuti is also known as Hru-Behutet or Hru-Behdet, because it was the main center where Kamitic clansmen first created iron tools and weapons. Since he is the owner of iron tools and weapons, anytime there are tools and weapons around he is present. Anything that involves breaking or cutting calls him because Hruaakhuti is first and foremost a hunter, but hunters don't just hunt for food. They also hunt for wealth and glory, which is the drive behind innovator and entrepreneurs. As a result, he can be seen on the fields with farmers toiling the earth but also with villagers band together to defend themselves against invaders and tyrants. He is the scalpel that guides the surgeon's hand and the individual that sacrifices him or herself in order to save others. Wherever there is bloodshed, typically Hruaakhuti is present, which is why it is advised that menstruating women stay away from his implements, until their cycle has run its course.

Hruaakhuti governs the spirit warriors that protect you. He is your personal security officer or personal bodyguard, but this doesn't mean that he owes his allegiance to you. So don't think that you can go out do wrong and he will defend you. Not hardly. He expects you to do what is right. When he comes into your home and he sees anything suspicious or alarming. He will signal you to take cover, while neutralizing the threat like the fictional character John Creasy played by Denzel Washington in the 2004 remake *Man on Fire*. Like Creasy, your Hruaakhuti is all about justice and protecting you from those who would try to do you harm. It is not his job to be your best friend. His number one priority is to justice and in order to serve justice. He focuses on removing all obstacles. Point blank, he is about getting ridding of obstructions so that everything can flow smoothly.

Some equate Hruaakhuti to an uncontrollable wild fire but I don't think this is entirely accurate. There have been cases where wild fires have been known to consume everything in its path and go around or stop short of certain areas. This in my opinion was Hruaakhuti that

186

stopped the wild fire. The wild fire on the other hand was Set. Set is the one who is the author of chaos and confusion. Nothing that Set does makes any sense or rather there is no logical explanation behind it because it is usually ego-driven. This is why Set is the author of war. Hruaakhuti is the netchar that appears to restore balance and order by any means necessary in order to bring an end to Set's chaos. The difference between Set and Hruaakhuti is that the latter walks with Maat. So you see, if we were using fire to symbolize him, it is because of Maat, Hruaakhuti is a like a controlled fire, while Set would be a fire or any uncontrollable force of nature maxed out to the extreme.

Hruaakhuti is a foot soldier. In the legend, Hruaakhuti fights Set but is unable to truly defeat him for this purpose. It isn't until Hru comes into the picture that the allies of Osar are able to defeat Set. This from my experience is because Hruaakhuti has no concern for wellbeing once the adrenaline kicks in. He simply jumps into the fire, whereas Hru tends to think more about the overall picture. In an actual war, Hruaakhuti would be more concerned about winning the battle, while Hru would be more concerned about winning the war. Hruaakhuti's motto would be more like "Fight to the death!" while Hru's motto would be more like, "Live to fight another day!" You see, Hruaakhuti who is older than his nephew, taught Hru how to fight, but Hru is a strategist and that is the difference between the two. It can be said that Hru learned from consequences.

This is why you see Hruaakhuti show up time and time again, on the battlefields. He is the daring fireman rushing into a blazing fire to save others. Hruaakhuti protects us so that when we engage in arguments and conflict we can arrive at a solution quickly. When there are no paths of opportunity, he cut a path and creates a new way, which is why he is also the patron of inventors and entrepreneurs.

Hruaakhuti's colors are dark red or red and purple. I have on occasion seen him as the color green but like rusting iron quickly turn to reddish orange. He is fond of the foods that all hunters are fond of like wild game such as venison. He also likes red beans, black beans, chili and hearty spicy foods. Roasted foods like yams, corn and potatoes are also his favorite from my experience, including rum, vodka, gin and cigars.

His totem can be feral dogs, falcons, lone wolves, mountain lions and bears. You will know when Hruaakhuti shows up because he usually looks like someone or something you don't want to mess with and he is usually found roaming alone. He is the unmentioned hero that doesn't get the credit he deserves, but still fights just the same behind enemy lines.

Maat: Guardian of the Way (Maa)

Purpose: Protect Against Calamity
Colors: Light Blue and White
Sacred Number: 2
Day of the Week: Thursday
Sacred Space: Place next to Hruaakhuti (unless otherwise specified)

Some people believe that Maat being a feminine principle is weak, soft spoken, and dainty and that Hruaakhuti has to protect her like a mindless brute. My experience has taught me different. Hruaakhuti is not a mindless brute but more like the executioner or the dispenser of justice. While Maat is the one standing right beside him giving the sign thumbs up or thumbs down.

Maat's human archetypes are the police. Years ago before the police were called cops, the heat and the pigs, they were called "the Law" and they were the true protectors of the law. This is why John the Baptist is also equated with Maa, because he was the one believed in Christian lore to represent the Law. This is the reason Jesus had to be baptized because the significance of this act was that no one is above the law.

It is Maat that pulls you over because your taillight doesn't work or you were exceeding the speed limit. It is Maat you pray to not to give you a ticket and ask "Please be merciful?" Not Hruaakhuti, because when you get to him. Mercy or your "luck" as they say has run out. Maat is the inventor of the three strikes and you're out policy. She represents the first two strikes and Hruaakhuti is strike number three.

188

It is often believed that because Maat's scales symbolize balance that she is a judge. Not from my experience. If you have done wrong by breaking the law and you know that you were in the wrong, but you did it to justify the means. Then you ask for forgiveness and promise from that moment walk a straight and narrow path. Maat may show up and be merciful by giving you a warning. But, if you go back and do the same thing, knowing it is wrong. Maat will not only throw you in jail but introduce you personally to Hruaakhuti and to whomever else you offended.

Maat is envisioned as being a beautiful and a mature woman that has seen her share of ill. She knows the evil that people can inflict upon others when they are consumed by their egoistic views and selfish needs. So she vows to protect others from being taken advantage of and abused ever again. Like Hruaakhuti, Maat has a strong sense of justice. This is why everyone influenced by Maat always begins by wanting to prevent something from occurring usually because of some past event. The problem is that if they do not remember their purpose. They are swayed by Set and their ideal purpose easily turns to wrath and vengeance. This is why no kid grows up wanting to be a corrupt police officer. It all begins with them wanting to protect and serve but somewhere along the line they lose their way. Corruption sets in because they forget their purpose. Then after people cry out afoul that is when they realize that instead of being part of the solution they set out to create. They have become part of the problem.

This is why Maat has a close affinity with Djahuti because without him, she would be taken advantage of. The reason is because Maat is very idealistic and she dreams of everyone getting along peacefully. Djahuti is the one that brings her back to the physical world, while not shattering her dreams, so that both the physical and spiritual perspectives can become a reality.

Other idealistic individuals overseen by Maat are mathematicians and scientists, like Albert Einstein. According to history, Albert Einstein never suspected that his theories and work would be used in war. He was simply interested in understanding the universe in order to make the world a better place. It was because of the events that took place in his native homeland that made him an outspoken advocate against war, but he continued to cling to the ideals that science is to be used to advance humanity.

Maat is the netchart that makes us feel compassion for others and their plight. She is the one that appeared so that we can contribute our monies and other services to help at charity events, but she won't be made a fool. It is because of Djahuti, she brings order into our life based upon biological, physiological and spiritual means. When Maat sees that there is no biological, physiological or spiritual backing for a specific action or behavior, she will view it as being a deviation and perversion. This is because she sees the action or behavior as being a threat that will eventually lead to the destruction of the family, the clan and society as a whole. This is why self-development and self-mastery was highly encourage in Kamit and behaviors like kidnapping, substance abuse, addictions, homosexuality, incest, murder, stress, theft, sorcery, etc. were seen as deviate behaviors due to the lack of biological, physiological and spiritual principles provided by cultural traditions.

Maat protects against these types of calamity by introducing us to our ancestral traditions so that we do not self-destruct and can weather the storm of dogma, peer and societal pressures, based upon the survival of life. Maat is aware that we have made mistakes in our life, but expects that after if we see the truth, that we strive to overcome our conditionings and shortcomings.

She is fond of simple foods like fruits, nuts, wild berries, corn, cornmeal and water. She will accept a cigar on occasion but she does not seem to be openly fond of them. She also will accept a shot glass of rum or whiskey, and even a mug of beer. Unlike Oset and Nebhet, Maat is a bit rugged and she doesn't mind getting dirty and grimy. She still considers herself to be a lady and conducts herself like one, but she is a bit rustic, country, or a sort of down-to-earth type of feminine spirit, that enjoys lite and earthy stews made of beans. One can easily see her wearing a sky blue skirt but be careful she might have pistol on her side or a rifle strapped along her back. A lot of Native American aakhu especially females, identify with Maat, as well as frontier women.

Sokar: Our Wounded Healer

Purpose: Obtain and Maintain Perfect Health
Colors: Purple, Indigo, Black, Brown and sometimes White
Sacred Number: 13
Day of the Week: Saturday
Sacred Space: Place on the het (unless otherwise specified)

As I have stated in my other works I have several personal stories that I can share about Sokar. Sokar is described as being an old man (some say woman) that walks around cemeteries. He is also seen as being a beggar or derelict, but all of this is a disguise that masks his true power. His Hebrew name is Jehovah Rapha, which means, "The Lord is My Healer."

To work with Sokar we have to understand that sometimes we have to learn the hard way. Sometimes we have to experience affliction, grief, misery, pain and suffering, in order to humble ourselves, slow down and really see what matters. Sokar reminds us of this fact because he is the wounded healer that helps us to see that one's power doesn't come from superficial things.

Most tales about Sokar always begin by reminding us how he was once a prosperous and affluent individual. He was either once a ruler, like the orisha Babaluaiye, a wealthy man like the biblical Job, or a prominent individual like Saint Alejo. If he wasn't a wealthy individual then, he was a beggar that was near the rich like Lazarus in the parable told by Jesus. Whatever the case, the story is always the same, by some fluke of nature or twist of fate, he trades places and becomes poor, inflicted with illness and/or is casted out by those he believed were loyal, like the fictional character Louis Winthrop III played by Dan Akroyd in the 1983 comedy *Trading Places*. It is only after much longsuffering that Sokar makes his triumph return.

The truth that Sokar always tries to convey to us is that he is not the bringer of calamity, illness, poverty, etc. These are all conditions that come about when we identify with our Set and the things that enhance our ego. Sokar in every role always makes a triumphant return and reclaims all of the riches and glory that he lost. When he realizes

191

that the things of the material things are not what make him who he is. It is the divine power dwelling within him that does. This is why he experiences some form of loss because it is his divinity, not the things of the world that can save him.

This is a difficult lesson for many of us to learn but for those who learn it. They can attest that Sokar has helped them to overcome illness, poverty, etc. because they coped with their misfortune and through maturity and the determination not to die. Sokar helped them to bury their anguish or bad habit at the gates of a mystical cemetery and leave their misery behind, so you can be transformed and resurrected into a fuller, richer and more complete way of life.

Sokar reminds us to appreciate what we have and never to take anything for granted especially our health. He is offered colognes and perfumes, out of appreciation and a reminder of how things use to be. He is fond of rum, dry wines, cigars, flat ales, seeds, grains, simple foods like beans, rice, corn, barley, etc. He helps you to keep things in perspective so that you never forget how things use to be.

Exercise 7:
Creating Sacred Space for Your Guardian Spirits

Figure 16: Spiritual Pot for Netcharu with Guides

All spirits need a place to reside and the second shelf of the *het* (spirit house/altar) is reserved specifically for your netcharu. Along with this, your netcharu would most likely prefer a pot to define his or her personal space. Besides providing a residence for the netcharu, the pot is basically a living amulet consisting of spiritual forces that have been awakened and empowered in order to improve the life of its owner. The pot itself consisted of an odd number of ingredients that may or may not include precious stones, dirts, herbs, rocks, plants, sticks, shells, lodestones, coins for attracting money, dice for luck and anything else that the spirit requested. The possibilities are endless and for this reason I cannot write specifically what it is that you need without personally knowing you or being familiar with your spirits. So, below are general instructions to aid you in this process. The idea is that when you make a pot for the netcharu, in essence you are creating a charm. For instance, you are not building an Npu, you are making a charm designed to help bring you general luck. Therefore, there are certain things that you have to do to keep it charm so that it continues to bring you general luck and so on.

For those of you wondering how this particular system came about, it has to be remembered that when the Europeans shipped the Africans to North America. Unlike the captives shipped to the Caribbean and South America who managed to bring sacred objects belonging to their sacred spirits from their homeland to a foreign land where practicing priesthood members had already begun modifying their tradition to meet the new circumstances, thus making it possible for the various Afro Caribbean and Afro Latin traditions to exist today. It is because of the valiant efforts made by these brave individuals that it is said in places like Brazil and Cuba; some of the orishas came to the Americas to be with their children. Early African Americans however were not as fortunate.

Early African Americans had no sacred objects to cling to and no community with priests and priestesses. What sacred rites and traditions they had were destroyed when slave-owners on a whim decided to sell their slaves, which separated the family as the member was shipped to another part of the country. The only thing early African Americans manage to retain from their homeland was all inside of their heads. Because a picture is worth a thousand words, as stated earlier the Kongo Cross became the most important and valuable glyph. Through it they were able to inscribe it on the ground, on pottery and basically anywhere they pleased to create new contacts with their sacred spirits. Relying on memories from the past and borrowing from the surrounding cultures, they found a way to rekindle this connection, which led to the creation of spiritual altars that acted as spiritual doorways and attracted "any spirit" that was willing to work for its keep sort of speak.

Now, I am aware of the different spiritual systems that use spirit pots but this is the spiritual technology I discovered draws upon the early African American memory jar tradition and their use of buckets, which they have been using for quite a while. While the Native American aakhu Black Hawk typically requests to be placed in a bucket. I remembered when I was in Jacksonville, Florida meeting a spiritual worker that had another Native American aakhu on a clay platter specifically for blessing money and patrons that came into her store, whose name wasn't Black Hawk.

194

There is also mention in *The Spiritual Churches of New Orleans: Origins, Beliefs and Rituals of an African American Religion,* by Claude F. Jacobs and Andrew J. Kaslow, of various spirits that resided in buckets like Kind Uncle, Aunt Peggy and Little Brother. Two interesting things about this practice, which reveals the origin of the tradition, is that the word "uncle" appears to be a corruption of the KiKongo word "nkisis" (medicine/charm), which is a container (incorrectly called fetishes) that served as resting places for various spirits. The second is that some equated Kind Uncle with the Hruaakhuti equivalent Catholic Saint George, who defeated the monstrous dragon[31].

The beauty of this tradition, which reveals the creativity of our aakhu, is that the pot can be made out of any container such as a bottle, jar, etc. It is extremely versatile, which is the reason it continues to survive. For instance, a conch shell provided it is has been legally obtained makes an excellent pot for Oset and can be inconspicuously placed in one's dwelling, without anyone ever knowing that it is the home for a spirit.

Returning to our subject at hand, the pot basically consists of all of the netcharu's personal objects and gives them (and the spirits that work under their guidance) the space needed to do their work. Everything on the pot or inside it is both owned by the netchar and used as a tool to assist them in completing a task in KAMTA or is under their direct influence. For instance, my Npu (Sebek or Anubis in Greek) besides having a decorated statue in his honor has a red and black flashlight, a knife, and a compass among other things. As I had mentioned in my previous works, my Npu likes to travel in style and enjoys "bling" because one day I went outside of my house and found near the doorstep a red and black-chromed toy hummer. Coincidence? I think not considering I also found a red and black toy four-wheeler. Who else plays with toys and their colors are red and black; No one but Npu.

---

[31] Dragons in Kamitic thinking were thought to be monstrous snakes, but they symbolized people ruled by snakes or the lower division of the spirit – sahu, hence evil people.

195

At this time I will like to mention that your netcharu will ask for various objects like this, and if you can get them by all means do so. Your netcharu are aware of your shortcomings and will not ask you to do something that will endanger your life or the life of others. Again, this was the purpose of the previous exercises. There are a lot of spirits in our universe and just like people some are good and some are bad. It is your job regardless if you choose to work with them or not, to determine which spirit you choose to listen to. But, when a spirit asks for something that you can easily obtain, which doesn't compromise your principles. Your sahu will ask...

"How is that possible? What does this have to do with me? How will this help me to get what I want, etc.?"

My advice when these questions arise is to ignore them and do not entertain them at all. It is a trick from Set to deter you from creating a miraculous way of life. You have to learn that one of the important keys to creating a magical way of life is recognizing your limitations. You will not understand or be able to explain everything that occurs in KAMTA, which is why it will always remain a mystery. Just like you can't explain why when your flick a light switch the lights come on, which is why it is best to accept that some things must remain a mystery and move on. Not only is it better this way, but it makes life more interesting.

To create the pot is a very lengthy process, but a very personal and powerful one. Here is where your aakhu come into the picture, which is why I stressed that they must introduce you to the netcharu. If not you will end up having a spiritual pot with no "spirit", no "anointing." It will not inspire you or anything, so you have to be introduced by your aakhu.

1. Begin after your aakhu have introduced you to the netcharu by recognizing the purpose or the goal that you want the netchar to achieve in your life. This is the purpose of building the pot. Contemplate on the purpose and see how the netchar can assist you if necessary.

2. Go shopping for a ceramic clay pot like the ones found in nurseries. The pot should be at least five inches in width and large enough to place objects on the outside and inside. Don't worry about if the pot is not very big. In the future, if the netchar's influence grows and it will request a large pot. For Hruaakhuti, you will need to purchase a cast iron pot or cauldron.

3. While at the store look for items that symbolize the netchar's purpose. For instance, if making a pot for Hru whose goal is to help attract success to you. You might want to get a money clip or anything symbolizing macho, strength, victory, etc.

4. Take the pot home and the objects related to the purpose and clean it.

5. Next take some black acrylic craft paint and paint the inside of the container. After it dries, paint an equal arm cross with white paint. The equal armed cross combined with the ring of the dish forms the Maa Aankh. The floor of the dish painted black symbolizes KAMTA, thus indicating the mystery manifesting itself in the physical. In the color of the netchar paint the sigils associated with the netchar's. (Note for Hruaakhuti don't use paint. Instead draw the cross with white chalk. He is not overly fond of liquids touching him.)

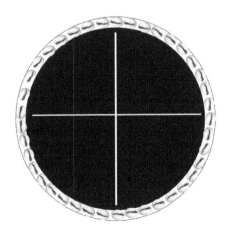

Figure 17: Possible Pot Design for Nebhet

6. On the outside of the pot, paint it the colors pertaining to the netchar of your own design. When it dries, attach the objects you purchased relating to the netchar on the pot using an adhesive. Nebhet's pot would be painted on the outside all yellow (or gold), yellow and green or yellow and pink design with maybe river shells, gold rhinestones, small mirrors, used to attract love and attention. The pot should be visually appealing to you. If it does not stir your feelings of interest and seems uninteresting. It certainly will not stir the feelings of your netcharu and their spirits. Keep in mind you are trying to draw this energy out of KAMTA into the physical.

7. When everything is in place. Write the purpose of the pot on a brown piece of paper using a pencil. For instance, if for success. Then write a note to Hru, "Your name/Success" nine times. Regardless what the desire is write it nine times. Then place the petition in the center of the cross and pour sand on top of it for the netchar to stand. If you have a statue or any other icon of the netchar. Stand it up in the sand.

8. Make the sign of the maa aankh over the pot, and then spray the pot three times with a mouthful of rum to give it life. Followed by a mouthful of cigar smoke for breath.

9. Place a candle in the sand and light it. Then say a prayer to Nebertcher (this can be the Lord's Prayer or a prayer in your own words), asking God to bless your pot so that it be used for self-empowerment and personal development. While doing this you can take your hands and lay them on the pot as you would lay them on a person for blessing and healing. Next, say a prayer to the netchar asking them to help you in the chosen objective. Tell the netchar in your own words that the pot is for them and the spirits willing to work with them, to make their home. Anoint the rim of the pot from right to left with olive oil or frankincense. When the candle has extinguished itself place on the het or its designated space.

198

Note: To dismantle Your Netcharu pot. Simply thank the spirits for helping you in your works. Then tell them to return peacefully from whence they came. When you feel the life of the netcharu pot seem to leave, then you can begin dismantling it physically. Natural items can be returned to the earth while icons and other manmade items can be washed in saltwater and either kept with other supplies or donated to a thrift store.

Visitors to Your Netcharu Pot

The more you work with your netcharu the more you will notice particular characteristics about them. You will find that they rarely move from the space you have put them like an individual living in a physical home. They will also have visitors. Some of these visitors are spirits that will pass through your space just to get some strength or guidance. Then they will move on, but most of your netcharu visitors will be your aakhu, specifically teaching, mystical and Native American aakhu. For instance, sitting outside my Sokar pot is St. Lazarus and San Alejo, both who are prominent figures that taught me about perseverance, resilience and steadfastness in regards to health and healing.

Communicating with Your Netcharu

To work the pot, treat the netchar like you would any other living being. The same way you wouldn't want anyone to barge in your home, you should barge into his or hers. If I have done my weekly ritual of honoring the aakhu and netcharu, I always begin standing in front of them and knocking either on the space itself or on the floor of the het. Then I say, "Hetepu (Netchar's name)", light a white candle and then I begin to tell them what I need or what I am having a problem with. Next, I wait for a response to intuitively come to me. If no response comes to me immediately it is because I know that they are working on the issue. In that event, I thank them still and allow the candle to burn out; this way the candle is continue to feed it energy. Occasionally, I may get the hunch to set another light for them. If this is the case and I am able to do so, I will do it.

Usually, an answer comes to me through this process from some synchronistic event. If not, it comes to me in a form of a dream. This is why it is important for you to know how your spirits communicate to you, so that you know how messages come to you. When they have answered a petition, I may give them a candle, a shot of rum or something special like food or flowers.

It must be remembered that you are not obligated to following their advice. This is your life and you are responsible for it. You should always be skeptical about any suggestion that you receive. The only way to learn if the suggestion is correct is by trying it.

I am always grateful for whatever assistance I get. When something happens unexpectedly, I say aloud "Thank you" for whatever spirits assisted in opening the way for the miracle to occur. If a particular netcharu helped you to obtain a goal or is working on it, you will know because you will see a sign that comes from them.

Collecting for Your Netcharu

Occasionally, you will be inspired by your aakhu to obtain specific items for your netcharu from nature such as dirts (earths), rocks, sticks, etc. For instance, if you may be walking down a path and a particular rock catch your eye. Greet it. This does not have to be aloud. Afterwards, pick it up and put in its place a few pennies. Anoint it, as you would do any other charm. Based upon its similarities place it with the netchar.

Working with Your Netcharu

Working with the netchar is not much different from communicating but I chose to make it a separate passage because your success depends upon you. The first thing that should be kept in mind is that because this is a living entity, it has to be fed on a regular basis. The netcharu should be fed after you have done the ritual to honor your aakhu (See Appendix A). To feed the netcharu simply set a white light for them and offer a shot of beer, rum, whiskey, coffee, water or whatever the netchar's preference, while thanking them for filling their purpose. For instance, to feed your Hru you would knock three times to wake them up. Then you offer a white candle, a shot of rum, while saying "Thank you Hru for, success, fame, confidence, vitality, increased health, vitality, charisma and protection."

Now, to work with the netcharu open communication with them as you have been doing by knocking three times, greeting them and lighting a candle. Next, explain to them what you want or the goal that you are trying to achieve. For instance, if you were working with Sokar for healing, you would explain to him why you want to be healed because you enjoy running, doing physical activity, etc. You never go to the netcharu complaining about your lot in life because it sends a signal to the spirits that maybe you aren't happy and are ready to leave this realm. You always approach them with the objective in mind that you want or need to do something in order to live, be happy, be at peace, be successful, etc.

Once you have firmly in mind an image of what it is that you want. Tell the netchar about it and explain your expectancy of the goal. Then, thank them for helping you to achieve the goal. Because the netcharu have passed on to KAMTA so long ago, they forget how events in TASETT work. They forget that while time is not important in KAMTA, TASETT is influenced by time. So when money is needed

201

to pay the rent, a miracle needs to be created. That being said, you need to repeat this ritual for a total of nine days or however long it takes for you to impress it upon them what you want. This means that if you are doing a ritual asking for Sokar's assistance in healing your body. Your business and your religion is for healing, which means it is your job to remind him that you want to run (if that is your purpose). This also implies that during the day in your daily life. You need to keep this image on your mind to constantly remind Sokar, so that he believes you are serious. When Set visits you with ideas of doubt and uncertainty, you need to replay this image in your mind's eye and if necessary say, "Thank you for perfect health" or whatever it is you are trying to achieve.

Remember, that once you impress what you want into KAMTA, you have to physically act on your faith. Asking for a job and not looking through "Help Wanted Ads" but expecting a job to come to you, more than likely is not going to happen. You have to do something that will help make your goal a physical reality.

This same ritual can be adapted and used for obtaining short term goals such as improving grades, getting into an exercise routine, dieting, breaking habits, etc. because essentially you are creating a new habit for your sahu to follow.

Now be warned, remember Set's objective in our life is to test us, so he will tempt you and try every way possible to discourage you. This is the reason when we decide to go on a diet, as soon we make the decision to stop eating chocolate. Someone out of nowhere brings double chocolate brownies or hot cocoa with mint. If that doesn't happen then he will tempt you with some advertisement in a magazine or some commercial on television. Stay strong and know the reason he has won before is because you didn't have an ally. Now that you have a spiritual ally and understand with the netcharu you can create new dreams, new habits and new memories. Know that you will be successful and it will be wise to simply ignore and if necessary avoid anyone and anything that speaks of doubt. Do not listen to arguments against your goal nor entertain what people believe or don't believe you can accomplish. When any ideas of doubt appear to you, simply cast this sin aside. Don't read anything that speaks and teaches contrary to

202

your goal. Do not even speculate on how any of this is possible. Remember, no one knows what occurs in KAMTA because it is beyond the living. Let your aakhu and netcharu concern themselves with how things get done. Your job is to work your faith by remaining focused on your objective.

Avoiding Getting Spooked (Self – Hexed)

A self – hex occurs whenever you unintentionally focus on a thought for too long and it betrays you. This usually occurs because an idea passes across your awareness as a suggestion and before long you find yourself affected by it. Another term for this phenomenon is 'spooked' and the suggestion can come from anyone especially authority figures, our friends, the television, internet, etc. It can even come from yourself if you don't watch your words or thoughts.

Now, I don't want you to become paranoid, because this phenomenon doesn't occur all of the time, but people that have weak wills due to fighting ailments, suffering from overstress, etc. are particularly vulnerable to these types of influences. Usually we all get spooked every now and then, we just don't think about it. The most common ways we get spooked is whenever we see a disturbing image especially while eating. We find the image disgusting because it out of the norm. Another form of being spooked is when someone tells us that something bad is going to happen if we engage in some activity. This is different from a verbal curse because usually the individual spooking us has a general concern for our wellbeing, like our parents. The thing is that they just don't know that this is what they are doing. For instance, I remember my mother told me one day when I wanted to sell my artwork that she didn't want to see me peddling my work on a street corner. She meant well and I understood what she was saying was that she didn't want me to have to struggle to make a living. But, my sahu interpreted as my mother not being proud of my artwork or me. It took a serious minute (long time) for me to work up the courage to do my artwork and sell it to people and it was because my sahu got spooked.

One of the most common ways our sahu gets spooked is from people of authority. I noticed this when I went to the doctor for my checkup. One day, I was in a pleasant mood as I went to the doctor, but while there. I found myself fighting to keep a positive outlook on my condition and it was because I was reading all of the medical advertisements. I noticed that after I read the advertisements, brochures and other uninformative literature they had scattered around the waiting room. That the more I read, the more I began to wonder if this was a condition that I had or if I may need this prescription; It wasn't until I caught my breath and relaxed that I realized what was going on. It was this experience that taught me that sometimes, the less you know, the better off you are.

In this information age, we feel sometimes that we need to know everything but really we don't, especially when you are trying to recover from an illness or achieve a specific goal. When you start paying attention to all of this useless information, your sahu will soak up this information and if you are not careful, will have you dwelling on these images, which will later influencing your action and behavior. This is why now when I go to the doctor. I take some music and a book or something to keep my sahu entertained. I don't focus on the medical stuff because I am not a physician and I don't have any training or desire to become one. So I don't need to know everything my physician knows. I only need to do one thing and that is, tend to my business by minding my spirit, to prevent the child in me (my sahu) from worrying.

This practice will come in handy because when you work with your netcharu, especially if it is your first time. You will have to learn how to leave issues in their hands and have faith that all will work out. This is difficult for a lot of people especially if they don't have knowledge of self and can recognize when their Osar or Set is leading them. As you can see, this is the purpose of the previous exercises that were covered throughout the book.

You will also find this helpful because you will learn as you build a rapport with your netcharu that they correspond to various aspects in nature. Some of the similarities you will find might be helpful because it pertains to your destiny, but others correspondences will not and might be more of a hindrance than anything. For instance, keeping in mind what I said about the need of knowing medical information.

Hruaakhuti the warrior patron for instance, corresponds to our immune system, but if you are trying to build a rapport with him. You will find it hard to fathom how our immune system corresponds to getting a job or how Nebhet, who is said to correspond to sexual organs relates to increase in finances. The problem you see is that there is a loss in translation between the metaphorical language and scientific reasoning. It is another form of being spooked where you have been blocked intellectually.

Making Deposits

Because our sahu at times tends to make us worry or what is sometimes called, "lust for results." You may need to place your request and an offering there in an area that is commonly frequented or in a place in nature. For instance, it is a common practice that anything you want to attract something to you, place it near your front door or under your doorstep. To keep something close to you, place it in the back of the house or your backyard. To diffuse and dissolve a matter, throw it into the crossroads. To get rid of an influence, throw a symbol of it into running water such as the gutter or flush it down the toilet. To destroy a things influence, burn a symbol of it. To attract joy and laughter, place it in park where children frequent, and so on, which are all subtle ways of impressing ideas onto your sahu.

Making Sacred Oaths

The word maa aankh is composed of the Kamitic words maa meaning, "righteousness, truth, order, balance, law, holistic, justice, etc." and aankh, which means "eternal life, to swear an oath." Thus, the maa aankh depending upon its use in speech can be a noun meaning "the order of life" or it can be verb meaning, "to make an oath to live righteously."

As we have seen in the previous chapters, Set is not exclusively an outside force but an energy dwelling within associated with the lower division of our spirit – the sahu. No one can totally purify himself or herself of Set's influence (sin), because no one is perfect. Perfection can only be achieved after death. However, we can learn how to control and keep Set from overthrowing our lives by making an oath with the netchar.

To make maa aankh, you will begin communication with the netchar as normal by knocking three times, lighting a candle, etc. Then, tell the netchar of the habit you are having a problem breaking for instance, cussing, smoking, overeating, excessive drinking, etc. It doesn't matter what your character weakness is. The purpose of this is to break negative behaviors. Next, ask the netchar to assist you overcoming the destructive behavior. Finally, make an oath that every time you break the oath that you will offer them a dollar.

This is a very powerful technique similar to a swear jar with the added difference being, that the netchar is watching your back and will ensure that you keep your promise and honor your oath.

Accessing Power from the Divine

Our aakhu as you have read are God's messengers. They are the ones that we can talk to about our problems and will help us to achieve our goal by showing us how to access the Divine's power. But, this is not just about getting what you want. Our ancestors remind us that we have a responsibility to each other and ourselves.

When we find that we have a host of problems in our life especially when it comes to trying to get something we want. The problem lies with Set, which means that we are not doing what we should to keep or maintain the blessing. Everything in life is about power but in order to will this power you have to take responsibility for it. It is like fire, fire has the ability to create and destroy, but only a responsible individual knows when to use it correctly. If everything in life was approached from this perspective, we would see that only a responsible young man and woman should be married according to our ancestral values because marriage makes one responsible for the lives of each other and the offspring produced from it.

If a blessing or goal has not been yet received, the fault does not lie with those in KAMTA, but it should be looked upon from the perspective that the aakhu don't believe you are ready to take on such responsibilities. If you really want to obtain the goal then you should ask them to help you to become responsible so that you can obtain your goal. Then step aside and allow the Divine to flow through you. Whenever you feel like you cannot do something or don't know how. Ask and step aside. This is how you allow the whiteness of Hedjet to guide the redness of the Deshret.

In Conclusion: The Divine Plan

I hope that you can see that the host of problems that exist are in life are all due to Set, but Set is not some impish character creating havoc in our life. Set symbolizes the negative and destructive aspects of our lower self (our ego) that we need to overcome. Set is the energy or spirit that brings the calamity, chaos, confusion, storm, war, etc. into our life, but this is not without reason. If we had never fallen or experienced hardship, problems, troubles, etc. we would not learn how to overcome these obstacles through the power of God. If we look at the problems that we have from a natural perspective based upon our egocentric views. We will see our problems as curses and succumb to the belief that God is punishing us or allowing Set to curse us because of something we have or have not done.

But, we look at the problem from our supernatural perspective based upon the higher spirit within us. We will see that God has not cursed us, but allows Set to exist in our life so that we can reach our greatest potential. It is by Divine Plan that we triumph over evil, overcome obstacles, etc. when we come face to face with adversity. The problems in our life exist, so that we can seek out the Divine and discover for ourselves, how to overcome the dilemma in order to help others and us.

It is when human beings are pushed in a corner and have reached their physical limitation that we discover our divinity. Like a diamond in the ruff, Set is the extreme pressure that we all encounter in life forcing us to discover the Divine's Power. We will never discover the power of the Divine if we give into our ego's whims. It is only by opposing our eternal enemy that we discover it. One way to do this is by making your problem not about you, but about others.

Consider this, a couple has an autistic child and if they looked at their life as it being a curse and asked why would God bless them with an unhealthy child. They allow Set to defeat them but, if they looked at their life and saw it from a different perspective and as an opportunity to discover their greatness. They may seize the opportunity and use it to learn how to teach other parents how to help autistic children. As you can see, if they never had an autistic child and learned how to help their own child, they would not have learned how to help others to help their children.

This is why God blesses us with our aakhu (ancestors) to help us to learn that the Divine's Power is not meant to benefit a few but all. Such a change in consciousness only occurs when we begin to take responsibility for our own salvation and seek the power of the divine for our self. When we look beyond the dogma, we will see that the various religious paths are just that – religious paths that all lead to the Divine based upon one's cultural perspective. We have to understand that we all essentially want the same things from the Divine – happiness, peace, love and prosperity. We all are just taking different roads to achieve it. There is no right or wrong way to serve God. There is only one way and that is the way that works for you without infringing upon the lives of others. This is the first step to creating a miraculous way of life.

While anyone can discover the power of the Divine, this spiritual power is not going to be bestowed upon us by us living any way we desire. The same steps an individual has taken to become a physician are the same steps any student desiring to be a physician must take also, because God doesn't play favorites. The same rules or principles exist for one as they do for others. If not, it would not be fair and God would not be just. To understand this principle, imagine you go to work everyday and at the end of the week you get a paycheck. You have a next-door neighbor that works at the same job, but he doesn't go to work everyday. Instead he watches television and does whatever he wants. At the end of the week he gets paid the same amount of money that you get paid. Is that fair? Not hardly. This is why the role of our ancestors is to provide a spiritual model and offer advice on how we are supposed to live.

Our aakhu are aware that we have all had problems that we had to overcome. That no one is perfect and we have all made mistakes out of spiritual ignorance or due to us not knowing the correct way to tap into the power of the Divine. This doesn't mean that we should give up and declare ourselves a victim. We simply have to get back on the horse, try again, and keep trying until you get it. This is the reason why you are here, so that you can learn how to purify your soul of all of the impurities – anxiety, fear, guilt, worry, etc. – that you have acquired while living in the physical realm.

The actual spiritualization of our soul is what spirituality is all about and when you are attuned to your ba (your higher spirit/higher self) or Osar. You will know when you messed up. You will feel bad or dissatisfied. You will be able to talk to your Osar (and aakhu) and ask, "Why do I feel bad?" and your Osar will tell you, "Because you shouldn't have done that." So, the next time you are in a similar situation you talk to your Osar, which cause you to grow spiritually and become a mature individual.

Because "no man is an island" and you shouldn't function as if you are in a vacuum, it should be remembered that even though I discovered this system out of sheer necessity. It was because I didn't have specific resources available to me. As a result, one of the objectives of this system as it was given to me, was to reintroduce me back to my family and community. This is because as I wrote in Maa Aankh volume one, my family saw me as being an outsider. Today, although most of my family still does not understand the path that I have chosen. They are on the other hand, willing to listen and have even seen some of the benefits as I have helped them to see the loss of respect for elders, the aimless search to become a man or woman because of no rites of passage program, and so on. This made me realize that the true outcasts are those who choose to be by going against cultural ethics and values.

Kamitic spirituality is not supposed to be practice in solitude but within a community because it is not intended to just benefit one or a few individuals, but an entire society. This is how spiritual growth occurs from a traditional African setting. It is by helping others, while they help you. That being said, I encourage you after you see the benefit of this tradition, to make this a way of life by practicing it daily. This means not just using it to improve your life, but using it to help others. Offer blessings to your loved ones. Erect simple shrines at parks to ensure that all whom visit will be blessed and that Set's influence it driven out. Bless your home, apartment complex, neighborhood, streets, etc. It is not necessary that you make a scene doing this because you are not doing this to satisfy your ego. You are doing it to resurrect and restore the kingdom of Osar.

From here I encourage you to create a spiritual community that supports your efforts and encourages others. Form groups so that you can learn from others and encourage others to learn from you. Join with others in exploring the mysteries and learning how to implement them in each other's life. Don't just make this group an organization for studying books and discussing theories, because these groups tend to eventually become ego driven (based upon how much an individual remembers) and drive away people who could benefit from the practice. Instead be sure to include in your study group charitable activities. For instance, one Saturday out of the month instead of meeting to discuss principles, activate them by volunteering at a meal center (soup kitchen). You might instead decide to clean up a vacant lot or volunteer at a nursing home.

Next, take steps to create a spiritual community by scheduling events and programs that will help to improve the community at large such as blessing rituals, drumming and dancing classes, community services and divination and journeying sessions. Because this is not a religion, but a cultural way of life, encourage others in the community to learn how they can benefit from their ancestor's wisdom.

In addition to this, try to address the needs of your community. As a Child of Osar, it is not necessary for you to wait for some leader to emerge in order for you to build up your own community. As the saying goes, "No one is coming. God sent you." So, start by creating community gardens with the hopes of eventually building a local farm and community market. Find ways to create jobs and build your community up by using your skills and talents for others. It should be remembered that the Kamitic priests and priestesses were not just clergymen and women. This was one of their roles.

210

In time, there will be people that may approach you for spiritual assistance such as a blessing, divination, aid in doing a ritual such as setting a light, etc. I remember, Papa taught me that no one is supposed to use something that the Divine has made available to us all for free to make money from. This is the reason he worked as a mechanic by day. This means no charging for divination sessions, for praying for an individual, etc. They can however accept donations but there should not be a set fee for these services. This is how Set corrupts an individual and ends up becoming all about them and his or her ego.

The old way it was done is that an individual is supposed to pay for the supplies used to perform a ritual and that's all, which means they pay for the candles, herbs, charms, etc. You can at any time refuse to assist an individual especially if they ask in doing something unethical.

The point of this discourse is for you to understand that problems will always arise because it is a part of life, but the way to deal with them is through wisdom so that all can be prosperous and live in peace. We can accomplish anything once we stop seeking solutions from outside of ourselves and begin to go within. The more we use this tradition to help others, the more we help ourselves the more we will see that we are interconnected and truly one family.

Appendix A: Suggested Practices

Drawing the Maa Aankh

Everyone and everything has a maa aankh all depending upon perspective. For instance, a tree's roots can be seen as coming from Amun Ra in KAMTA, while its branches can be seen as stretching towards Ra in TASETT, and so on. A simple practice that can used to invoke the power of this symbol is to draw it by following the seven steps below:

Step 1: Begin by drawing from left to right a horizontal line, while saying "Nyun."

Step 2: Draw an intersecting vertical line from the bottom across the horizontal line, while saying "maa."

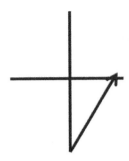

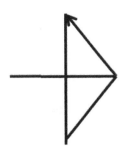

Step 3: From the arm of the vertical line draw a diagonal line to the right of the horizontal line above, while saying "Shu."

Step 4: From the right side of the horizontal arm, draw a diagonal line to the top of the vertical line, while saying "Tefnut."

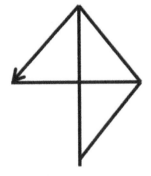

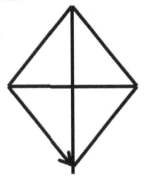

Step 5: From the top of the vertical line, draw a diagonal line to the left arm of the horizontal line, while saying "Shu."

Step 6: from the left arm of the horizontal line, draw a diagonal line to the bottom of the vertical line, while saying "Tefnut."

Step 7: Complete the maa aankh by drawing from the bottom of the diagram a counter clockwise circle connecting all of the points. While doing this say the following invocation, "Es Khepera, Ra, Ra Atum en Amun Ra," which is a salutation to Nebertcher that means "Greetings/Hail to the One that Governs Birth, Life, Death and Rebirth."

Praying to God

God is Nebertcher – the Lord of All Things, which means that God is everywhere. The reason most people do not see this and feel disconnected to God is because God in many Western religions has been relegated only to residing in churches and temples. This is the reason so many people after attending religious services digress back to their sinful behavior of cussing, arguing, committing adultery, etc. as soon as they leave church. It is because while most may believe that God is everywhere, they feel as if God only is watching them while they are attending church. Their Set clearly has sabotage them.

Believing that God is everywhere means seeing that God can be found anywhere because the Spirit of God or Rau is the indescribable

214

and unimaginable power of life, and it is in everything. God is in everything including the things we see and do not see like the air we breathe. This means there is no place that can hold or contain God because only God's power can be felt, which is why there are no symbols to accurately describe and explain what and who God is for God is known and unknown at the same time.

Accepting this means that God can be prayed to anywhere because God sees all. God is the only one that is worshipped and prayed to. Everyone else is simple honored. God can be worshipped amongst others but can also be prayed to when you are not with a group. In fact, it is when we are alone that we are really able to hear the Voice of God. Pray to God wherever you are and express your gratitude for the blessings you have. It is not necessary for you to bow down on your knees. You can pray to God while you are warming up your car. You can pray to God while you are cooking. You can pray to God while walking alongside a stream or pray before you fall asleep and begin to dream. Basically you can pray to God anywhere and since prayers to the Most High are a personal affair. It is not necessary for you to share your prayer with others or speak aloud. It doesn't matter where you pray to God, but you should get into the habit of doing so every day to express your thanks and ask for blessings. In return you will feel a sense of serenity and strength as you come into the presence of God.

Honoring the Aakhu

Your aakhu (ancestral spirits) are the spirits that God has placed by divine design to serve as intermediaries. It is your aakhu you talk to about problems within your family and other problems occurring in your life. They are the ones that will help you to resolve these issues. To enlist their aid you have to honor your aakhu and netcharu on a weekly basis.

The purpose of honoring your aakhu and netcharu (guardian spirits) on a weekly basis is to attract and ensure that you have blessings, good luck, health, etc. Traditionally Monday or Friday are the days most in the Afro-Diaspora perform this ritual but you choose whatever day is the most convenient for you. I personally prefer Saturday since it

215

is an optimal day for doing ritual cleansing. Assuming you have already cleaned the space, have an altar built and have glasses of water and offerings in place.

1. Begin by standing in front of your altar and tracing the Maa Aankh in the air.
2. Knocking on the altar three times.
3. Begin to get yourself ready to enter into KAMTA (trance) by continuing to stand or sitting in a straight back chair, and saying a prayer of your choice. Because the Lord's Prayer is a powerful, general and familiar prayer, it is typically used in African American spirituality for this purpose.
4. Slow your breathing and relax while praying. Once you have entered into a trance state, thank the Almighty God, Nebertcher – Lord of All Things, for all your blessings and the things you are grateful for.
5. Ask God to bless His servants, your aakhu with wisdom, power and continue to purify their soul, so that you may benefit from their experience.
6. Light the candle (and incense if available), and then welcome your aakhu as such: "Welcome and thank you aakhu." State what you have offered them like, "I offer you coffee, cologne, a shot of rum, etc."
7. Finally, tell the aakhu what you want using command words, "Bring me prosperity. Bless me with your wisdom. Increase my wealth. Protect my family. Remove evil away from me, etc." End by saying "Thank you or Tua-u (Thanks/Thank you).

The glasses of your het aakhu (and any other dish) should always be cleaned, when you do this weekly rite, so as not to allow decay to set in.

Remember, if you have netcharu pots you need to feed them immediately after honoring your aakhu.

Feeding the Netcharu Pot

To feed the netcharu simply set a white light for them and offer a shot of beer, rum, whiskey, coffee, water or whatever the netchar's preference, while thanking them for filling their purpose.

Appendix B: Selected Bibliography

Amen, Ra Un Nefer. *Metu Neter, Vol. 1: The Great Oracle of Tehuti and the Egyptian System of Spiritual Cultivation.* Khamit Media Trans Visions Inc. 1990

Ashanti, Kwabena F. *Rootwork and Voodoo: In Mental Health.* Tone Books, 1987

Bockie, Simon. *Death and the Invisible Powers: The World of Kongo Belief.* Indiana University Press, 1993

Budge, E.A. Wallis. *An Egyptian Hieroglyphic Dictionary Vol. I and II.* New York: Dover Publication, 1978

Budge, E.A. Wallis. *Osiris & The Egyptian Resurrection, vols. 1 & 2.* Dover Publications, 1973

Gadalla, Moustafa. *Exiled Egyptians: The Heart of Africa.* Tehuti Research Foundation, 1999

Gomez, Michael. A: *Exchanging Our Country Marks: The Transformation of African Identities in the Colonial and Antebellum South.* The University of North Carolina Press, 1998

Harner, Michael. *The Way of the Shaman.* Harper One; 10 Anv. edition, 1980

Ions, Veronica. *Egyptian Mythology.* Littlehampton Book Services, 1986

Jacobs, Claude F. and Andrew J. Kaslow. *The Spiritual Churches of New Orleans: Origins, Beliefs and Rituals of an African-American Religion.* The University of Tennessee Press, 1991

MacGaffey, Wyatt. *Custom and Government in the Lower Congo.* University of California Press, 1970

MacGaffey, Wyatt. *Religion and Society in Central Africa: The BaKongo of Lower Zaire.* The University of Chicago Press, 1986

Moore, Derric. *Maa Aankh: MAA AANKH: Finding God the Afro-American Spiritual Way, by Honoring the Ancestors and Guardian Spirits.* Four Sons Publications, 2010

Moore, Derric. *Kamta: A Practical Kamitic Path for Obtaining Power.* Four Sons Publications, 2011

Moore, Derric. *Maa: A Guide to the Kamitic Way for Personal Transformation.* Four Sons Publications, 2012

Myss, Caroline. *Sacred Contracts: Awakening Your Divine Potential.* Three Rivers Press, 1 ed. 2003

Raboteau, Albert J. *Slave Religion: The "Invisible Institution" in the Antebellum South.* Oxford University Press, 1978

Shafton, Anthony, *Dream-Singers: The African American Way with Dreams.* John Wiley & Sons, Publishers, 2001

Smith, Theophus H. *Conjuring Culture: Biblical Formations of Black America.* Oxford University Press, 1994

Thompson, Robert Farris. *Face of the Gods: Art and Altars of Africa and the African Americas.* Prestel, 1993

Thompson, Robert Farris. *Flash of the Spirit: African and Afro-American Art and Philosophy.* Random House, 1983

Thorton, John. *Africa and Africans in the Making of the Atlantic World, 1400-1800.* Cambridge University Press; 2 ed., 1998

Williams, Chancellor. *Destruction of Black Civilization: Great Issues of a Race from 4500 B.C to 2000 A.D.* Third World Press, 1987

Young, James T. *Rituals of Resistance: African Atlantic Religion in Kongo and the Lowcountry South in the Era of Slavery.* Louisiana State University Press, 2007

INDEX

aakhu, 68, 80, 81, 82, 83, 85, 86, 87, 88, 89, 90, 94, 95, 96, 97, 98, 100, 101, 102, 103, 104, 105, 106, 107, 108, 109, 110, 150, 151, 161, 162, 164, 165, 168, 169, 185, 189, 190, 191, 194, 195, 198

Aan, 143

ab, 35, 46, 47, 48, 49, 50, 51, 52, 57, 61, 65, 70, 81, 108, 127, 136, 153, 174

Afro-Diaspora, 85

amulets. *See* charms

Amun Ra, 47, 48, 62, 67, 70, 93, 98, 102, 163

ancestor, 84, 86, 87, 100, 101, 165, 205

anointed, 3, 9, 102

Anubis. *See* Npu

archetypes, 151, 162, 169, 183

Ausar. *See* Osar

Auset. *See* Oset

ba, 35, 36, 37, 39, 46, 57, 58, 61, 63, 69, 70, 71, 74, 77, 81, 111, 112, 113, 117, 141, 153, 155, 156, 158, 169, 204

blessings, 6, 7, 24, 31, 77, 84, 104, 113, 124, 139, 147, 156, 157, 205

Calling, the, 77

charm, 135, 137, 142, 143, 146, 147, 149, 188, 190

cleansing, 137

conscious. *See* ab

cosmogram, 8

Crown. *See* Deshret crown, Hedjet crown and Pschent crown

curandera, 137

curse of Ham, 12

Deshret crown, 17, 73, 139

devil. *See* Set

Djahuti, 59, 97, 143, 174, 176, 177, 178, 184, 185

ego, 37, 38, 42, 43, 44, 45, 56, 58, 61, 69, 70, 74, 90, 116, 117, 167, 182, 186, 205

El Nino de Atocha, 172

Evil Eye, 131

figa, 134

gods, goddess, not, 159

good angels, 80

guardian angels, 36, 79, 80, 81

haints, hants or haunts. *See* Aapepu

heaven, 61

Hedjet crown, 17, 75, 98, 139

hell, 61

herst, 139, 140, 141, 142

het (spirit house/altar), 188

higher division of the spirit. *See* ba

higher self. *See* ba

Holy Ghost, 3, 4, 36

homosexuality, 185

Hru, 47, 59, 60, 84, 99, 127,
    139, 145, 159, 164, 165, 173,
    174, 175, 176, 177, 178, 181,
    182, 192, 193
Hruaakhuti, 59, 84, 147, 169,
    174, 175, 180, 181, 182, 183,
    184, 190, 192, 200

Khepera, 47, 48, 148
Kongo, 13, 14, 15, 155
Kongo Cross, 13, 87, 189
Kongo-Angolan, 13

limpia, 137

Maat, 169, 182, 183, 184, 185
Mahalia Jackson, 12
Mal de Ojo. See Evil Eye
Malcolm X, 72
Malochia. *See* Evil Eye
miscellaneous charms, 137
money offering, 108

Napoleon Hill, 151
Nebhet, 59, 93, 145, 171, 174,
    178, 179, 180, 185, 192, 193,
    200
Npu, 59, 99, 166, 169, 170,
    171, 172, 174, 190

orishas, 36
Osar, 36, 37, 46, 47, 55, 58, 59,
    60, 63, 67, 68, 77, 80, 87, 93,
    100, 107, 111, 112, 114, 115,
    116, 117, 123, 124, 136, 139,
    148, 156, 159, 160, 164, 165,
    167, 169, 170, 171, 173, 174,
    176, 177, 178, 179, 182, 199,
    204, 205

Oset, 58, 93, 146, 149, 171,
    172, 173, 174, 177, 178, 179,
    185

Parks, Rosa, 79
prayer warriors, 13
Protective Fragrances, 135
Protective Jewelry, 135
Protective Pets, 136
Protective Plants, 136
Pschent crown, 59, 76, 139

Ra, 171
Ra Atum, 47, 48
Rau, i, 9, 29, 30, 31, 32, 33, 34,
    35, 37, 38, 65, 72, 74, 122,
    126, 128, 130, 131, 136, 156,
    157

sahu, 35, 38, 39, 40, 41, 44, 46,
    49, 51, 54, 56, 57, 59, 60, 61,
    63, 64, 69, 70, 71, 80, 81, 94,
    95, 105, 112, 127, 132, 133,
    150, 153, 155, 156, 157, 158,
    177, 191, 197, 198, 199, 200
Set, 44, 45, 55, 56, 57, 58, 59,
    60, 61, 63, 64, 66, 69, 80, 81,
    93, 111, 112, 115, 117, 118,
    121, 123, 125, 126, 127, 128,
    129, 130, 131, 132, 139, 147,
    151, 159, 163, 164, 170, 173,
    174, 175, 176, 177, 179, 180,
    181, 182, 184, 186, 191, 197,
    199, 205
sharp object. *See* miscellaneous
    charms
shu (the Kamitic yang), 16
sin, 46, 50, 52, 153, 197

slavery, 11, 12, 13, 15, 84, 85, 86, 87, 88
Sokar, 167, 186, 187, 194
spirituality, 11, 12, 13, 20, 21, 71, 85, 98, 143, 169, 204
subconscious. *See* sahu
superconscious. *See* ba

tefnut (the Kamitic yin), 16
Thomas Edison, 152

ushabti, 164

Yoruba, 36, 84, 167, 174
Yowa. *See* Kongo Cross

Author's Note

Thank you for allowing me to share my experience, story, and methods that I have found that worked for me with you. I hope that it empowered and improved your life the way it has touched mine.

If you enjoyed the book and have a minute to spare, I would really appreciate an honest review on the page or site where you purchase the book. Your review is greatly appreciated because reviews from readers like you, make a huge difference in helping new readers find practical spiritual books like this one.

Amazon Review: https://amzn.to/2Y30nA1

1 SoL Alliance.com: http://bit.ly/2Ggz5fh

Thank you!

Derric "Rau Khu" Moore

Other Books by the Author:

MAA AANKH Volume I:

Finding God the Afro-American Spiritual Way,

by Honoring the Ancestors and Guardian Spirits

Kamta: A Practical Kamitic Path for Obtaining Power

Maa: A Guide to the Kamitic Way for Personal Transformation

MAA AANKH Volume II:

Discovering the Power of I AM Using the Shamanic Principles of

Ancient Egypt for Self-Empowerment and Personal Development

MAA AANKH Volume III:

The Kamitic Shaman Way of Working the Superconscious Mind to

Improve Memory, Solve Problems Intuitively and Spiritually Grow

Through the Power of the Spirits (Volume 3)

Honoring the Ancestors the Kemetic Shaman Way:

A Practical Manual for Venerating and Working with the Ancestors

from a God Perspective

The Kamta Primer: A Practical Shamanic Guide for Using Kemetic
Ritual, Magick and Spirituality for Acquiring Power

En Español: Maa Aankh Volume I:

Encontrando a Dios al Modo Espiritual Afroamericano, Honrando a los

Ancestros y a los Espiritus Guardianes

Neter (God) Got Your Back!

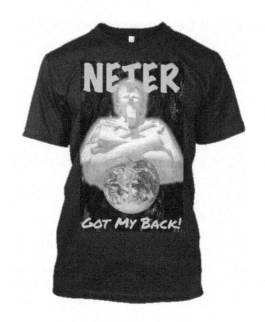

Purchase your empowering, enlightening and uplifting MKBN tees, hoodies and caps today at 1SoLAlliance.com

For more books on religion, astrology, numerology, chakras, prayer, reiki, self-help and metaphysical supplies, visit us at:

www.thelandofkam.com

www.1solalliance.com